Soul Food

A LAYMAN'S STUDY *of* HEBREWS

JEFFREY LEATH

outskirtspress

DENVER, COLORADO

To Reta, Mallory, Kyle, and Philip

Table of Contents

PREFACE
To My Children

Reta and I were surprised and blessed when we learned that we were going to be the parents of triplets. After many visits to Johns Hopkins Hospital in Baltimore, Maryland, in the mid to late 1980s, our dream of having our own family was realized. Our children, Mallory, Kyle, and Philip are now grown. Gone are the days when Daddy could do anything. Daddy used to be the funniest person known. Today the kids and I joke about how their responses to me have gone from the giggling "Oh, Daddy" to an annoyed "Oh, Father!"

Gone, too, are the times when family events provided the social life. When the middle school years began, so did the social life away from the family. When the college years began, we were fortunate to be together at holidays. I remember being the number one man in my daughter's life, but for several years now, I realize that she has been talking more privately with Mom.

I don't remember when the boys got older. I don't remember when they started shaving or grew to be taller than me. It's certainly harder to tickle them now. I remember when they wanted to look like me and do what I do.

It is needless to say that gone are the days of *Barney* and *Mr. Roger's Neighborhood*. There are no more new drawings to place on the refrigerator. We have recently placed a "save the date" magnet on the refrigerator, as Philip will be getting married soon. We long ago stopped keeping track of height. Happy Meals were replaced by Big Macs or double cheeseburgers, which have been replaced by dinners out with their significant others.

I'm not sure, but if I were honest, this project may just be an attempt to assure myself that I performed my responsibility as a Christian father when I had the chance. It could be more for my sake than for the sake of my children. But no matter if it's for them or me, I am concerned for my children. I had always heard from my mother that no matter how old I got, she would still worry about me. I understand that now. No matter how old my children get, I will still be concerned for them.

As a father, I'm concerned about my children's character, their behavior, their health, their relationships, and their salvation. When they were young, we could teach them about Jesus. Frankly, we could teach them about anything. Now they think and reason on their own. I often wonder if I impressed on my children that which I consider to be the most important values. Did I teach them discernment? Did they understand? Am

I an example of what I taught? I guess that's where this study comes into play.

The most important thing that I want my children to know is that *the* most important things are eternal. Store up treasures in heaven! Look toward that city whose foundation cannot be shaken! For this, you must realize your need for Jesus Christ as Lord and Savior. It is God's grace through Jesus the Messiah that makes salvation possible. It is grace only. One cannot add one good work to grace. Because of His grace, we receive His righteousness, and His grace and righteousness are manifest in our character. Trials, temptations, and persecution will occur, but we count it all as joy because these will help us grow spiritually. And finally, we will live in this world that rejects Christ. But there is hope! God is in control. Our salvation and eternal life with Him are assured. Through Jesus, we have direct access to our Heavenly Father.

The following pages are my own personal study of Hebrews. I am merely a layperson. My study is a compilation of many scholars and theologians. I take no credit for interpretation of any passages of scripture, thus footnotes are provided. It is my hope that as you look upon this book, you understand the most important things in life that your dad wants you to know: Jesus, grace, grace manifested, and God is in control. You belong to Him!

INTRODUCTION
Christ, the Passover Lamb, Fulfills the Law

When studying Hebrews it is best if one can place them-
selves, as a Jew, in the first century church. Hebrews, being
a sermon or a letter, was targeted to Christian Jews who were
tired of waiting for Jesus's return, as well as experiencing the
persecution that comes from being followers of a man who
was crucified on a Roman cross. As we study Hebrews, we'll
see how the Preacher uses Jewish history to show that history
points to Jesus fulfilling the law and the prophets.

The book of Hebrews encourages its audience to view Jesus
as the all-sufficient, powerful redeemer who completes
God's program to bring us to Him. Reviewing the Passion,
we can learn how Jesus did not abolish the law and the
prophets; *He fulfilled the law's requirements.* For example,
there is still need for a sacrificial lamb, but needing to sacrifice a lamb each year is made void as Jesus is the one and

only sacrificial lamb. There is still need of a high priest, but when Jesus died, the curtain in the temple was torn and opened,so that now through Jesus our High Priest, we have direct access to God!

So to begin our study of Hebrews, let's practice having a Jewish mind-set. We begin our study with an introduction to the Passover. Of all the holidays and celebrations meaningful to Jews, Passover is the most important and is at the beginning of the Jewish calendar. Although this is not used in Hebrews, by reviewing Passover we get an idea of how Jesus fit into Hebrew history.

Easter Sunday

"Easter" is the English word for the Greek term *pascha,* which means "Passover." Passover was the first of three feast seasons. All Jewish males were required to journey to Jerusalem for a special encounter with and visitation from God. The Lord's Passover was on the fourteenth day of the first month at twilight (evening). Passover was to be a memorial to the Hebrews' deliverance from Egypt (captivity). This deliverance happened during the month of Nisan and represented God's first encounter with His covenant people.

I. The Death Decree

God gave Pharaoh every chance to let the Hebrews go, but with every plague, Pharaoh's heart grew more unyielding. The final plague was the decree of death on the firstborn male of every family (Exodus 11). But along with this decree, God gave specific instructions on how to be saved from this death.

II. Instructions

A. The lamb
Every man was to select for his household a lamb without spot or blemish, and no broken bones. He was to select this lamb on the tenth day of the month. This lamb was brought into his house for testing for five days to make sure there was nothing wrong with the lamb, that is, there could be no fault in this lamb.

B. Killing the lamb
On the fifth day, the lamb was taken to the doorstep of the house and killed on the third hour. It was cooked and eaten beginning at the ninth hour so as to be consumed by evening. The lamb's blood was then sprinkled on both sides of the doorpost as well as along the top of the doorpost. This was done at three o'clock in the afternoon on the fourteenth day of the month. The family then entered the house through the blood-stained door.

C. Eating the lamb
The entire lamb was to be roasted and consumed. Nothing could be left over for the next day. In preparing the meal, not one bone could be broken. To roast the lamb according to these instructions required that the lamb be placed on a spit shaped like a crossbar so its body could be spread open.

D. The temple

When the temple was built, instead of killing the lambs at the doorpost, the people would bring the lambs to Jerusalem and kill them at the temple. As time passed, it became difficult for the people in outlying areas to bring their sacrifice to Jerusalem. So the Levites began raising lambs for the Passover sacrifice right in Jerusalem and selling them at the temple.

The original intent was for these lambs to be set aside specifically for sacrifice. They were to be without fault. However, as time passed, rules for raising these lambs grew lax, and thus "bad" lambs were being sold in the temple. Thus, it wasn't just the merchants who upset Jesus when He entered the temple; it was the fact that dishonesty had infiltrated the raising and selling of the sacrificial lambs.

III. The Lamb of God

Jesus fulfilled the Feast of Passover in His crucifixion. Since the reason for His birth was to die as a sacrifice for our sins so that we could be saved from death, His life was predestined so that He would fulfill this purpose exactly as God had instructed the Jews to practice it for fifteen hundred years.

A. Approaching time

In order for the Jews to see Jesus as the Passover lamb, the final days were centered around the selection process, testing process, and death just as the lamb was selected, tested for faults, and killed fifteen hundred years before.

Jesus entered Jerusalem on the tenth day of the month. He was in Bethany six days prior to Passover, which would have been the ninth day of Nisan. John 12:12 records that the "next day" He made his way to Jerusalem. Beginning this day, Jesus was tested by the Jewish elite for five days. Remember how his authority was questioned, and He was asked trick questions but he could not be discredited? They could find no fault in this lamb. Pilot announced that he could find no fault in Jesus.

B. Crucifixion
On the fourteenth day, Mark's gospel tells us that on the third hour Jesus was nailed to the cross at the time the lamb was being prepared. John's gospel tells us that on the ninth hour, when people were feasting, Jesus bowed His head and gave up His spirit. To hasten death, so the bodies would not be on the crosses for the next day that began at 6:00 p.m., the Roman guards began to break the legs of the crucified. But when they came to Jesus, He was already dead. Thus, Jesus's bones were not broken.

IV. Beginning of Grace by Faith
Notice that Jesus instructs Mary Magdalene to "not hold on to Me, for I have not returned to my Father" (John 20:17 NIV). In this passage, Mary Magdalene was not just physically clinging to Jesus, but also the Greek terminology used describes her emotionally clinging to Jesus and attempting to reestablish a relationship with Jesus in person, here on earth.

Jesus's response to Mary Magdalene in John 20:17 (NIV) reveals that His relationship was now based on faith. Those who believed in Him as the Son of God would be righteous. Further, in John 20:29 , Jesus tells Thomas that "because you have seen me, you believed. Blessed are those who have *not seen, yet have believed.*"

V. The Jewish Calendar

The standardized calendar used today is known as the Gregorian calendar, named for Pope Gregory XIII who established it in 1582. This calendar is a sun or "solar" calendar because it operates on the principle of the earth revolving around the sun. The days on this calendar begin at midnight and last for twenty-four hours. As the earth takes approximately 365.25 days to circle the sun, an extra day is added every fourth year.

The Jewish calendar is a moon or "lunar" calendar based on the movement of the moon around the earth. The days on this calendar begin at sundown, approximately 6:00 p.m. and also last for twenty-four hours. It takes approximately 29.5 days for the moon to circle the earth. Since a year of lunar months lasts 354 days, an extra month is added to every third year. This month is called the intercalary month, and is twenty-nine days long. Because of the 11.25 days difference in the solar and lunar calendars, each Hebrew month may come in one or two Gregorian months.

VI. Sacred and Civil Calendars

The Jews have two concurrent calendar years. One is the sacred calendar based on the calendar year that God established when He brought them out of Egypt. The second is the civil calendar based on the Jews' agricultural season. Since Passover was the first feast celebrated and represented the first of the three major encounters with God (Feast of Pentecost and Feast of Tabernacles were the other two), the sacred calendar begins with Passover in the month of Nisan (March-April).

Sacred	Civil	Name of Months	Farm Season	Feast
1	7	Nisan (March-April)	Barley Harvest	Passover
2	8	Iyyar (April-May)	Barley Harvest	
3	9	Sivan (May-June)	Wheat Harvest	Pentecost
4	10	Tammuz (June-July)	Grape Harvest	
5	11	Ab (July-August)	Olive Harvest	
6	12	Elul (August-September)	Dates and Figs Harvest	
7	1	Tishri (September-October)	Early Rains	Tabernacles
8	2	Heshvan (October-November)	Plowing	
9	3	Kieslev (November-December)	Wheat and Barley Sowing	
10	4	Tebeth (December-January)	Winter Rains	
11	5	Shebat (January-February)	Almond Bloom	
12	6	Adar (February-March)	Citrus Harvest	
13	–	Adar Sheni	Intercalary Month	

Additional Thoughts

VII. Did Jesus Come Out of the Tomb?

1. The Roman Guard securing the tomb was a battalion of approximately four to sixteen soldiers protecting an area thirty-six square feet around the tomb. They were highly trained soldiers with weaponry unmatched in its day.

2. The seal on the tomb was the government seal. Anyone breaking the seal was liable to death. Thus, if the body was stolen or was taken by some other manner:

   a. How was the Roman Guard at the tomb penetrated?
   b. Why wasn't someone placed on trial for breaking the government seal?

VIII. Who Were the First to Recognize Jesus as the Lamb of God, the Sacrificial Lamb?

For this, we look at the Christmas story. The angels told the shepherds that the Savior has been born, the Messiah (Christ). "And this will be a sign unto you," i.e., this is the sign that you would recognize: the baby will be wrapped in rags (swaddling clothes) and lying in a feed trough (manger).

The shepherds would have recognized this sign as a sacrificial lamb. As their first job was to raise lambs for Jewish sacrifice, one of the first things they did when a lamb was born was to inspect it for being "perfect, without blemish." Any baby lamb that had the possibility of meeting these criteria was cleaned off, wrapped in rags, and laid in the feed trough. The shepherd(s) who took care of sacrificial lambs would know to take the ones from the feed trough and raise them separately. Thus, wrapped in swaddling clothes and lying in a manger would have been a significant sign to the shepherds.

IX. A Place to Lay His Head

There is one more point in this story that bears revealing, and it is the use of the word *kephalon,* a Greek term that means "to lay down one's head." This term is used in only two situations in the New Testament. The first is in Luke 9:58 (and Matthew 8:20), and the second is in John 19:30. In the first passages, we find Jesus is traveling and is confronted by a young man who tells Jesus that he will follow Him anywhere. Jesus says that just as birds have nests and foxes have holes, He has no place "to lay down His head." It is a different situation in John. In this passage Jesus is on the cross. He takes a sip of sour wine and states, "It is finished," and then He "lays down His head" and gives up His spirit. The only place on earth that Jesus had to lay his head was on the cross!

CHAPTER 1
Heavenly View

Hebrews, being a letter or a sermon, is directed primarily to Christian Jews. The author tells us in chapter 13:22 that Hebrews is a "word of exhortation." Dr. Stuart Sacks says these people were depressed or discouraged[1], and I believe if we could place ourselves in their positions, we would easily be able to see why. Christian Jews were referred to as *meshumadim*—traitors to Israel's faith. Shunned by family and friends, their life was difficult. The Roman government allowed any religious group autonomy as long as it obeyed the Roman laws and caused no trouble. But since Christianity had no ancient history, Rome merely recognized it as a branch of Judaism. Thus, Jews who converted to Christianity had no family or government with which to associate. Try purchasing anything in the marketplace when you are a known meshumadim. Thomas G. Long says that "it is important to keep the rhetorical situation of Hebrews in mind. The original readers

---

1   Dr. Stuart Sacks, *Hebrews Through a Hebrew's Eyes* (Messianic Jewish Publishers, 1995), page 9.

(or listeners) were not students in a class on world religions debating the relative merits of Judaism versus Christianity. They were disheartened members of a Christian community who had begun to lose their grip on their own beliefs and commitments. The Preacher responds to them as any good pastor would, by reassuring them that holding fast to their faith is truly the best way."[2]

As we begin our study, the first question may be: Is the message in Hebrews anti-Jewish? What does the Preacher of Hebrews want his audience to realize about Jesus and understand, that in Him is a "more excellent way"? The early church (as today) was watching for Jesus to return, expecting it at anytime within its lifetime. We need the Messiah to return! When will Jesus return and set up His kingdom? When will our lives get easier? The author of Hebrews is encouraging his audience to radically change its views of Jesus. Who is Jesus? He is no "supermonarch" but God incarnate! Focus on the greatness of our Lord and Savior. This revelation through the Son is not viewed by the Preacher as simply another progressive form of revelation (i.e., another revelation through the communication of a prophet). It is God's ultimate and climactic revelation of Himself through the Son[3] or "through Son."

1. Whom God appointed heir of all things ("appointment" signifying authority)

---

2   Thomas G. Long, *Hebrews: Interpretation* (Westminster John Knox Press, 1997), page 12.
3   J. Dwight Pentecost, *Faith That Endures* (Kregel Publications, 1992), page 45.

2. Through whom He made the worlds ("He ordered the ages" of time from eternity past through eternity)
3. Who is the brightness of His glory (not a reflection but an original, "is" signifying unbroken fellowship with the Father)
4. The express image of His person (all that is in the Father is in the Son)
5. He upholds all things by the word of His power. The word "upholding" has in it the idea of carrying something along to a designated end. Not only is the Son the One who is the architect of the ages, He is also the One who through the ages has been carrying creation to its designated end—by "power," implying "authoritative command that is consequently executed."[4]
6. He purged our sins and
7. Sat down at the right hand of the Majesty, which implies taking a seat of honor and authority at the completion of a specified work.

What is being implied, if not said, by the Preacher is that to reject Jesus Christ is to reject the one true God! In our first study, we looked at Passover and how Jesus is the Passover lamb. Does Jesus abolish Passover? No, Jesus fulfills or *completes* Passover. We can look at the Passover lamb and see that Jesus is a "more excellent" way or, in other words, a "more complete" way.

A second question that may arise is: Why does the writer begin his comparison with angels? What's so important about

---

4   Ibid, page 48.

angels? In Jewish belief, according to Exodus Rabbah 32:9 (Midrash on Exodus), "wherever an angel appears the divine presence of God appears."

What God communicates to us (Jews) is so vital that, according to the Talmud, "God will one day ask every Jew if he was diligent in setting aside a regular time for study. Israel's hope, it is reasoned, cannot survive if it is detached from that which God has communicated to her. Learning the words of God is critical, which is why study is so highly regarded in the Jewish community."[5]

In verse 2, we see in our English versions and translations that God has spoken through "a" Son, or "His" Son. It's worth noting that "Son of God" was not a new term for the Jews. "Sons of God" was a term used by the Jews in their references to angels:

- Names of angels in scripture: Sons of God (Hebrew *Bǝnê hā▢ĕlōhîm, bnei elim*—literally "Sons of Godly beings/powers," angels)
    Orthodox Jewish Bible:
        Psalm 29:1, bnei elim
        Genesis 6:2, bnei HaElohim
        Job 1:6, Bnei HaElohim
    Job 38:7, Bnei Elohim
    Luke 20:36, bnei HaElohim
- Exodus Rabbah 32:6—"If one performs a good deed, God gives that person one angel. If one performs two good deeds, God gives them two angels. If one

---

5   Sacks, *Hebrews Through a Hebrew's Eyes* ().

performs many good deeds, God gives that person half God's camp."

- Midrash Tehillim 88:4 (midrash on Psalms)—angels wait until all Jews finish their morning prayers and weave the prayers into a crown they place on God's head.
- *Malachim* meaning "messengers" was also another name for angels.

The original language of verse 2 has "no article or pronoun here with the preposition giving the absolute sense of 'Son.' Here the idea is not merely what Jesus said, but what He is, God's Son who reveals the Father."[6] Thus, "God spoke to us through Son!"

So God spoke through prophets or angels, but Jesus is even greater! Which of the angels did God ever call His Son? Only Jesus Christ is God. Jesus then, being God, is a more excellent way. Focus your attention, then Hebrews, on who Jesus is!

---

6   Dr. A. T. Robertson, *Word Pictures of the New Testament, Volume 5* (Broadman Press, 1932), page 335.

CHAPTER 2
1–4 Earthly View

The Hebrew most likely never forgot that he/she was of a race specifically chosen by God for a special task. Jews were very particular that their children should be well educated. It was their boast that the children were trained to recognize God as their Father and as the Maker of the world. They believed that "the world is upheld by the breath of children in the schoolhouse."[7]

Female students were taught at home to learn scripture that would help them as wives and mothers. Scripture of Jewish history, food preparation, holiday observances, as well as the Psalms, were required study and memorization.

At the age of six, a male would attend school for the first time. When he was able to read, he was given scripture passages to learn by heart:

---

7   Babylonian Talmud: Shabbat, 119b.

- The Shema (Hebrew for "Hear!"), Deuteronomy 6:4–9; 11:13–21; Numbers 15:37–41.
- The Hallel (Hallel means "Praise God!"), Psalms 113–118.
- The story of creation, Genesis 1–5.
- The Ceremonial Law, Leviticus 1–8.

In addition, the student had to search the scriptures for his "personal text," which began with the first letter of his name and ended with the last letter of his name. When reaching thirteen years of age, he was responsible for himself in his knowledge of and keeping of the law.

One continued his education past the age of thirteen to become a rabbi. This required continued study of the Old Testament ("Old Testament" to us!). Jewish rabbi teaching stated that for every passage of scripture, there were four meanings:

- The literal meaning,
- The suggested meaning,
- The investigated meaning through the grammar, syntax, and historical references, and
- The symbolic meaning.

This training continued until the age of twenty-one. As rabbis weren't allowed to take pay for teaching, a rabbi would learn a skill to support himself so as to not be a financial burden on anyone. Paul, for example, was a tentmaker.

What would education and learning from the spoken word look like? For example:

- Teffillin (phylacteries) from Deuteronomy 6:4
    » Sign of faith and devotion, small leather boxes containing parchment with passages of the Torah strapped on arms and foreheads each morning while reciting prayers.
- Kanoff (Greek *krespadon*) from Deuteronomy 22:12
    » Tassels sewn onto the corner of garments or worn later on a prayer shawl as a reminder of their relationship with their Heavenly Father.

We have the impression then that outward appearance showed devotion to God, and through generations this outward appearance became more important than the intentions of the heart to be loyal to God (see Matthew 23:5).

With all this in mind, we begin our study of the second chapter of Hebrews. If we can describe the first chapter of Hebrews as a chorus singing "All Hail the Power of Jesus's Name," then, with the second chapter, the chorus starts to sing "Take Time to Be Holy."[8]

The Preacher/author takes the audience from a heavenly view to an earthly view. What does realizing the truth that Jesus is "a more excellent way" look like? Will outward appearance reflect inward devotion, or would our hearts' convictions be manifested in outward behavior?

---

8   Thomas G. Long, *Hebrews: Interpretation* (Westminster John Knox Press, 1997), page 25.

To begin, let's first try to put ourselves in the audience's shoes. Many if not most of the audience came from Jewish education. The men were probably still wearing tassels (Jesus did; see Mark 5:25–34). But believing in Jesus as the Messiah at that time was much different than it is today. I don't believe we understand what they understood about the Crucifixion in their time and culture. "We easily forget that the central narrative of the Christian faith is, on the face of it, a deep embarrassment. Often we have turned the passion story into harmless sentiment and the cross into a piece of jewelry, losing touch with what early Christians painfully knew, that Jesus died in shame and that the cross is, to reasonable eyes, an inexplicable foolishness and a stumbling block to faith. No wonder the Preacher had taken such pains earlier to contrast the Son to angels, to emphasize that, when the full truth is known, Jesus the Son is higher than the angels."[9] There always was with the audience a danger that under the stressful conditions of persecution they would give up on their faith. So the Preacher's message is hold on to your faith! Remember, a true confession of Christ is priority one. We can see the shame of the Crucifixion; however, focus on the life that His death brings. God intends to give us salvation as a permanent possession; we must be all the more attentive to what He and others have said about it.[10]

To this end, the Preacher begins with nautical terms, telling the audience that "we must pay more attention so that we

9   Thomas G. Long, *Hebrews: Interpretation* (Westminster John Knox Press, 1997), pages 25–26.
10   Paul Ellingsworth, *Commentary on Hebrews, New International Greek Testament Commentary* (Eerdmans, 1993), page 135.

do not drift away." These terms "arrest the attention of the reader with a strong warning."[11] Using the Greek terms *dei* (must, literally "it is necessary") with the adverb *perissoteros* (more careful), followed by *prosecho* (pay attention) and *pararuomen* (drift away), the Preacher gives a word picture that it's not just logical but both logical and morally necessary. A pilot of a ship is steering the ship to port. There were no motors on ships! You miss the port and it may be days before you get another chance to dock your ship. It is a picture of a ship's pilot who is not only mindful of the swift currents but also convinced that there is no plan B. He *will* guide the ship to port on the first attempt despite the currents. The ship will then be "fastened to the seabed" (*prosechein*) to be kept from drifting.

When I think of striving to avoid carelessness, I'm reminded of Paul's message to run a race (I Corinthians 9:24–27). His analogy was of one training for games. The Greek term for "games" is *agonizomai*, the word from which we get our English words "agony" and "agonize." It sets in mind a specific task that involves training with the mind-set to achieve nothing less than first place. We earnestly heed the things that we have heard with the intention to achieve nothing less than being steadfast in our faith. We are earnest so that we will not give up or drift away. There is neither placing second in the race nor missing the dock!

Why be so determined? Angels gave the law through Moses

---

11   David L. Allen, *NIV The New American Commentary, Hebrews* (B & H Publishing Group, 2010), page 191.

(Deuteronomy 33:2, as well as Josephus, *Antiquities* 15.5.3; Acts 7:38; and Galatians 3:19). The law is binding, sure, and steadfast (*babaios*). How do we know it was valid? Because whenever one broke the law, that person received his or her just consequences. The terminology used shows a picture of one who *willfully* refused to listen or deliberately disobeyed, not from ignorance of the law. They received a just punishment. The word for punishment is *misthapodosia*, translated as "deserved" and used here ironically. It is a word that is used for a payment reward, but the payment here is punishment. So what we heard or what was given to us from angels is true. If we violate that truth, we can expect punishment as a consequence.

Now Jesus is greater than the angels, and in "these last days God has spoken to us in His Son." From this fact "it follows logically that the revelation delivered through the Son must be regarded with the utmost seriousness."[12] "How (*pos*) shall we escape" is rhetorical, having the force of a strong negative; "we shall not escape" such a great salvation (*soteria*). The word here, as in Hebrews 1:14, indicates salvation in its entirety: those who have been saved, those who are being saved, and those who will be saved. The thought here is that it denotes full, final, and complete deliverance from all sin and punishment. This salvation is so great "because it makes saints out of sinners!"[13]

---

12   William L. Lane, *World Biblical Commentary, Hebrews 1-8* (Thomas Nelson, Inc., 1991), page 37.

13   Robert Gromacki, *Stand Bold in Grace* (Kress Christian Publications, 2002), page 41.

Not only was it spoken by Jesus, but it was confirmed according to God's own will by

1. Those who heard it (Apostles)[14]
2. God Himself with them by
   a. Signs
   b. Wonders
   c. Various miracles
   d. Gifts of the Holy Spirit

"Signs" (*semeiois*) refers not so much to the sign itself but for what the sign stood for. "Wonders" (*terisin*) refers to miracles that are beyond explanation and render one astonished, amazed.

And so we have Jesus a "more excellent way" confirmed. This truth is inescapable. W. C. van Unnik says Hebrews 2:3–4 contain what one finds in the book of Acts in regard to preaching the gospel accompanied by signs and wonders. "Acts is the 'confirmation' of the Gospel of Luke. He (Luke) saw the overall purpose of Luke/Acts as presenting God's plan of salvation through Jesus and how that salvation was brought to those who did not see Jesus incarnate."[15]

As we started this lesson with hymns to describe the Preacher's words thus far, we can summarize how we may remain "careful not to drift" so to remain steadfast in our faith through one of Isaac Watts's hymns:

---

14   H. A. Ironside, *Hebrews* (Kregel Publications, 1932), page 33.
15   W. C. van Unnik, *The Book of Acts: the Confirmation of the Gospel* (NTS Publishers, 1960), pages 26–59.

Am I a soldier of the cross, a follower of the Lamb?
And shall I fear to own His cause, or blush to speak His name?
Are there no foes for me to face? Must I not stem the flood?
Is this vile world a friend to grace, to help me on to God?

—Isaac Watts (1674–1748)

We look back to the Greek term for "games" (*agonizomai*): those who profess a true confession of Christ may agonize over these questions almost daily.

CHAPTER 2
5–18—Earthly View

As we learned from the previous lesson, there was always within the audience the fear of danger that under the stressful conditions of persecution it would give up on their faith. So the Preacher's message is hold on to your faith! Remember, a true confession of Christ is priority one! However, be careful or you may drift away; we cannot ignore such a salvation! After stating evidence that history shows transgressions of the law (given through the angels) received just punishments, and that God Himself bore witness to Jesus's teachings through signs, wonders, and various miracles; then how or why would we ignore or neglect Jesus? Yet if Jesus truly sustains all things by His powerful work, why do we see Him weakly submitting to a cross of shame?

We know that the cross is a symbol for shameful behavior, deserving only a most hideous death/punishment. But we (Hebrew Christians) are tired of our status as "traitors of the faith," of being perceived as putting our faith in a man who could save others but couldn't even save Himself! There is a reason for this, further explains the Preacher: Christ's suffering was necessary. In the remaining verses of chapter 2, the Preacher will explain through the use of scripture that the world to come would be subject to Jesus's authority, not the angels. This authority over the world would come only after the Son was first placed "a little lower than the angels" (Psalm 8). The Preacher does not wish to argue that Jesus was just a tiny bit lower than the angels in the hierarchy of creation, that he came just to the edge of human life and dipped his little toe into the pool of suffering. Rather, he wants to claim that, for a brief moment in time, the eternal and exalted Son purposefully and redemptively plummeted to the depths of human suffering and weakness.[16] Not only this but also, as described in verse 10, it was *fitting* that the Son should suffer. This ("fitting") could be more confusing than enlightening!

The word "fitting" comes from the Greek *eprepen autoi* and can also mean "it became him" as a term of etiquette[17]—for example, one using "proper" table manners or a psychologist declaring one's behavior as being "appropriate." The idea of God suffering, or of a Divine One as being human, is difficult to understand. "Fitting" would not be a word that comes to mind when one thinks of God suffering.

Why was it fitting that Jesus become incarnate and suffer? The Preacher explains:[18]

---

16 Thomas G. Long, *Hebrews: Interpretation* (Westminster John Knox Press, 1997), page 36.
17 A. T. Robertson, *Word Pictures of the New Testament, Volume 5* (Broadman Press, 1932), page 346.
18 J. Dwight Pentecost, *Faith That Endures* (Kregel Publications, 1992), pages 61–71.

1. **Verses 5–9a:** God's purpose for man might be finally realized by the One who would take the title Son of Man.
   a. "What is your divine purpose for man as man?"
      i. Genesis 1:27–30. Administrative authority over creation, bringing all created things under his authority. Man brings all creation into subjection to God.
   b. Jesus, identifying Himself with the sinful human race, is able to fulfill the original purpose God stated for man (subjecting all things to Himself as Son of Man). This will be accomplished at His second advent.
      i. God's intention for man, but man sinned.
      ii. Jesus, God incarnate, fulfills God's intention for man and is brought to glory and honor.

2. **Verses 9b** and **17b:** Jesus became incarnate that He might taste death for everyone. Jesus's death was propitiation for sinful man.
   a. Becoming man is necessary for being an acceptable sacrifice to God on man's behalf.
   b. Jesus came into the world specifically for the purpose of dying.

3. **Verses 10–13** Jesus came so that through Him, God sees us with Jesus as brothers and sisters.
   a. All was created by Him, and all that was created was created for Him.
   b. Quotes from Psalm 22 and Isaiah 8.

4. **Verse 14**: He came to destroy the devil.
   a. Christ's death and resurrection was a divine judgment on Satan.
   b. Destroy, *hina katargesei*, does not mean to annihilate but to "render inoperative, idle, ineffective."

5. **Verse 15:** Deliver people from the bondage to fear of death.
   a. Judgment that follows death was cast on Christ on the cross.

6. **Verses 16–17a**: To become our High Priest, merciful and faithful
   a. Christ is the Mediator between God and man, and between man and God.
      i. Identifies with man's sufferings because He was man.
      ii. To manifest God's faithfulness, He must be God Himself.

7. **Verse 18**: To provide help to those being tempted for His sake
   a. God Himself cannot be tempted. He is not directly involved with sin, nor does He even indirectly involve sin in His tests (James 1:13), and
   b. God cannot be put to the test (Deuteronomy 6:16), so
   c. To identify Himself with man's temptations and tests, His incarnation was necessary.
   d. From J. Dwight Pentecost:

One question that might arise here is how Jesus, because He was sinless, could really understand and respond to our testing and temptations. We must recognize that Jesus, who is indeed sinless, does not identify Himself with us in our solicitation to sin. As I John 3:4 points out, sin is lawlessness, which is the tendency to declare oneself independent of God. This temptation can come from the sin nature within or from Satan without. Whatever the source, however, the testing is essentially the same.

At His temptation in the wilderness, Jesus was enticed to lawlessness. The temptation did not come from a sin nature within Him, but from Satan without. Therefore Christ understood the nature of temptation. We suffer because we live in an unredeemed body in an unredeemed world with an unredeemed sin nature with us. Jesus Christ did not have a fallen sin nature within Him but He did live in a corruptible body in this unredeemed world. He therefore was subject to the same sufferings to which we are subject, even without that fallen sin nature. As a consequence He can be sympathetic with us, a compassionate, merciful, and faithful High Priest. His sympathy is related to our testings, not to our sin. His sympathy does not depend on personal experience of sin, but upon the experience of the strength of sin as He did in His temptation, again in Gethsemane, and finally at the cross.[19]

With all this in mind, Hebrews (and us), He has done what no angel could possibly do. As great as the law given to Moses through angels at Sinai is, far greater is the revelation given through the Son!

---

19   Ibid, page 70.

ADDENDUM TO CHAPTER 2

5–18, the Preacher's Use of Psalm 8

---

1. **George W. MacRae, *Collegeville Bible Commentary, Hebrews*. The Liturgical Press, 1983, pages 14–15:**

The author again takes up the argument that Christ is superior to the angels, but from a new angle. In Chapter 1 Christ was superior as the Son of God; here he is superior because he is a human being. The argument again is based on Scripture as verses 6-8 quote Ps 8:5–7, but this time the author explicitly interprets the text he quotes. Two features of his interpretation are important. First, he understands the passage as referring not to humanity in general but to Jesus the man. And second, he reverses the meaning of the original psalm, which had said that God created human beings "a little lower than the angels." For Hebrews, Jesus the man is superior to the angels but was made "for a little while lower" than them in that he suffered death (v. 9). The subjection of all things to Christ still belongs to the future, but the process has begun with Jesus's exaltation to heaven after his death.

OF NOTE: The phrase "a little lower than the angels" comes from Psalm 8 in the Septuagint (Greek version of the Hebrew texts).

2. H. A. Ironside, *Hebrews*. Kregel Publications 1932, pages 37–38:

No angel will rule in that day. But He whose glory was foretold in the eighth Psalm will take the kingdom and rule in righteousness, for the certain place referred to in verse 6 is, as we know, Psalm 8:4–6, which is quoted here: 'What is man, that thou are mindful of him? And the son of man, that thou visitest him? For thou has made him a little lower than the angels, and has crowned him with glory and honour. Thou madest him to have dominion over the works of thy hands; thou has put all things under his feet.' If we turn back to the psalm we might not realize that it is Christ who is in view, particularly as we notice verses 7–8 where all cattle and wild beasts, as well as fowls of the air and the fish of the sea, are said to be subjected to man. It might look as though it is but a confirmation of the Lord's word to Adam the first, to whom He said, 'be fruitful and multiply, and replenish the earth, and subdue it: and have dominion over the fish of the sea, and over the fowl of the air, and over every living thing that moveth upon the earth' (Gen. 1:28). But we know well that Adam forfeited his headship through sin, and now in the eighth psalm that headship is confirmed to One who is call the Son of Man, which Adam, of course, never was. The use of the passage here in Hebrews makes it plain that it is the Last Adam to whom the psalm refers.

3. William L. Lane, *Word Biblical Commentary, Hebrews 1–8.* Thomas Nelson Publishing, 1991, pages 49–50:

In resuming the exposition the writer leads his readers to contemplate Jesus in his solidarity with humankind. The transcendent Son of God made the human condition, and especially its liability to death, his own in order to achieve for them the glorious destiny designed by God. That design, informs Ps 8, which speaks of the creatureliness and subordination of human beings, and yet also of the glory, splendor, and universal authority for which they have been created. Unfortunately, the promise implied by the divine intention has plainly not been fulfilled in humanity's limited dominion over nature. It actually appears to be mocked and frustrated by the presence of sin and death in the world. Nevertheless, it has been secured by Jesus, who took upon himself humanity's full estate in order that by means of his own redemptive accomplishment he might bring the vision of the psalmist to realization.

There is a profound note of anticipation in the OT teaching about humanity. The words of the psalmist look forward into the future, and that future is inextricably bound up with the person and work of Jesus.

4. John F. Walvoord and Roy B. Zuck, *The Bible Knowledge Commentary, An Exposition of the Scriptures by Dallas Seminary Faculty*. Scripture Press Publications, 1983, pages 783–784:

The author here returned to his main train of thought, the destiny of Jesus in the world to come. But now Jesus's intimate involvement through His Incarnation with those who will share that destiny was brought to the fore. It has been claimed that the Dead Sea Scrolls show that sectarians believed that the coming Age would be marked by dominion of Michael and his angelic subordinates. The statement here by the writer of Hebrews forcefully refutes this view. A portion of Psalm 8 was now quoted. While the psalm as a whole is often read as a general statement about the role of man in God's Creation, it is clear in the light of Hebrews 2:5 and the application that follows in verses 8b–9 that the author of Hebrews read it primarily as messianic and eschatological. In doing so he stood well within the New Testament perspective of the Old Testament, a perspective directly traceable to Jesus Himself.

Whatever might have been the general appropriateness of Psalm 8 to man's current standing in the world, in the view of the writer those words do not now describe the actual state of affairs. Instead, he affirmed, at present we do not see everything subject to Him. He was thinking here primarily of Jesus (Heb. 2:9). No doubt the familiar messianic designation 'Son of Man' (v.6) contributed to this understanding.

5. See also:

a. Clinton E. Arnold, *Zondervan Illustrated Bible Backgrounds Commentary, Volume 4.* Zondervan, 2002, pages 18–19.

b. Thomas G. Long, *Hebrews: Interpretation.* Westminster John Knox Press, 1997, pages 34–36.

c. J. Dwight Pentecost, *Faith That Endures.* Kregel Publications, 1992, pages 60–63.

d. Donald Guthrie, *Hebrews, Tyndale New Testament Commentaries.* InterVarsity Press, 1983, pages 88–89.

CHAPTER 3
Jesus Is Greater Than Moses

Jesus is greater than the angels. Now the Preacher wants to make a case again for Jesus, only this time he shows that Jesus is greater than Moses. By the end of these passages, however, his comparison of Jesus and Moses only reveals his warning to his audience, alluding to a direct comparison between those wandering in the wilderness and to his audience.

It is difficult to exaggerate the importance of Moses in Judaism and the veneration with which he was regarded. If reference is restricted to Jewish-Hellenistic texts, it is necessary only to recall a passage from *The Exodus* by Ezekiel the Tragedian (or Ezekiel the Poet who wrote plays around 300–200 BC), cited by Eusebius (historian). Moses is shown in a dream that God will place him on a heavenly throne and invest him with a crown and a scepter, the symbols of his unique authority. Although Moses is designated a priest only once in the Old Testament

(Psalm 99: 6), his Levitical background (Exodus 2:1-10), his ministry of the word and privileged vision of God (Exodus 33:12, Exodus 12:34–35, Numbers 12:7–8), and his service at the altar (Exodus 24:4–8) associate him with priestly functions. In this tradition, Moses is the supreme example of perfection in the sense of immediacy and access to God. If such views were the common property of men and women in dialogue with the Hellenistic Jewish community, they have bearing on the comparison of Jesus and Moses developed in Hebrews 3:1–6.[20]

In Sirach 44:23 through 45:5, Moses is described as "a godly man, who found favor in the sight of all and was beloved by God and people…(his) memory is blessed. He (God) made him equal in glory to the holy ones, and made him great, to the terror of his enemies. By his words he performed swift miracles; the Lord glorified him in the presence of kings. He gave him commandments for His people, and revealed to him His glory. For his faithfulness and meekness He consecrated him, choosing him out of all humankind. He allowed him to hear His voice, and led him into the dark cloud, and gave him the commandments face to face, the law of life and knowledge, so that he might teach Jacob the covenant, and Israel His decrees.[21]

The Exodus, in which faithful Moses led the Israelites from Egypt, and the subsequent desert wanderings constitute the most important era in the religious memory of Jewish people. In a broad band of the Old Testament as well as in

---

20   William L. Lane, *Word Biblical Commentary, Hebrews 1–8* (Thomas Nelson Publisher, 1991), page 74.
21   Sirach, from the Apocrypha, is used solely for historical benefit for this lesson on Hebrews chapter 3. *jl*

extra-biblical texts, the desert experience of the Israelites represents the premier symbol for disobedience to God.[22]

We all know the story. God said to Abraham that the land of the Canaanites would be given to Abraham and his descendants (Genesis 15:18–19). Just prior to this, God revealed to Abraham that his descendants (Israelites) would be strangers in a foreign land, they would be slaves and afflicted for four hundred years, but afterward they would come out with many possessions (Genesis 15:13–14). Through Joseph, Jacob and his family settled in Egypt, and through time (Exodus 1:8–14) his family (Israelites) became slaves to the Egyptians for four hundred years. Having heard the Israelites's cries, God sent to them a redeemer/deliverer to lead them out of the bondage of Egypt (Exodus 3:10–12). The nation accepted the release, or redemption, He provided through Moses; however, they weren't so accepting of Moses as God's ruler over them (Acts 7:34–35). The nation did, however, hold Moses in high esteem, as it was through Moses that the revelation of the law was given.

The law was the foundation for daily life.[23] The law provided means

- For fellowship with God

---

22 Clinton E. Arnold, *Zondervan Illustrated Bible Backgrounds Commentary* (Zondervan Publishers, 2002), page 23.

23 J. Dwight Pentecost, *Faith That Endures* (Kregel Publications, 1992), page 73.

- For acceptable worship
- For sacrifices through which one who violates the law might be restored to fellowship.

Even though Moses was faithful, the people "murmured" (Exodus 15:24 et al; note also what God says to Miriam and Aaron in Numbers chapter 12) and rebelled against the one (Moses) who had been their redeemer, ruler, and channel of revelation. The Preacher brings up the climatic rebellion at Kadesh Barnea (Numbers 14). Their unbelief resulted in a most harsh response from God. Here the Israelites were at the brink of going into their "rest" in the Promise Land, and God "loathed" them so much that this group (except Joshua and Caleb) was not permitted to enter the Promise Land. God was so angry He made a vow that those with unbelief would never go into the land of milk and honey. Turned around, they spent the next generation (forty years) in the wilderness—the consequence of disobedience and unfaithfulness.

The Preacher wants his audience, who he refers to as "holy brothers" and "partakers of a heavenly calling," to "consider Jesus." Why these terms?

1. "Holy brothers" reminds them that holiness is a divine gift, not an intrinsic human virtue, not a sign of the church's moral stature but of how God gracefully puts the church to work in the world.[24]
2. "Partakers of a heavenly calling":

---

24   Thomas G. Long, *Hebrews: Interpretation* (Westminster John Knox Press, 1997), page 47.

a. "Just as Jesus was sent by God (the meaning of the term 'apostle'), the church is sent to the world as well (John 17:18). Just as Jesus is the 'high priest,' the One who ascends to the holy place on behalf of humanity, so the church has a 'priestly' ministry of loving service and compassion. Just as Jesus is the source and focus of 'our confession,' the church worships, teaches, and serves 'holding fast to our confession.'"[25]

b. "The church does not convene like a political party attempting to forge a platform or wrangle like a special interest group trying to muscle forth an agenda. Rather, the church seeks to listen to the Spirit, to discern where and how Christ is active in the world, and to become not managers of a religious organization but holy partners in a heavenly calling."[26]

3. "Consider"(*homologeo*) would be like grabbing a person from the lapels and saying "listen up and pay attention!"

"His house," "My household," and "the House of Israel" are symbols used for "God's people." In Hebrews we find that the Preacher tells his fellow believers to focus solely on Jesus's faithfulness, as Moses was also faithful "in all His house." This now becomes used architecturally, showing Moses was faithful in the house whereas Jesus was the greater as He is the builder of the house; God the Builder of everything. And again, Moses

---

25   Ibid, page 48.
26   Ibid, page 49.

was faithful as a servant; Jesus was greater as He is faithful as a Son. Servants work for a master yet a son is the representative of, or more aptly, a direct extension of the master.

Beginning in verse 6, the Preacher's comparison of Jesus to other beings or persons changes as he slowly focuses on "the house" past and present. Before we note the Holy Spirit's inspired words in verse 7 and following, we remember the Preacher's words leading up to verse 3 in chapter 2: "How shall we escape if we neglect so great a salvation?" If unbelief led to the wilderness and forfeiture of entering rest, then "take care, brethren…!" (verse 12)

So this chapter begins with a history reminder (not a lesson as it is well known by the audience) and ends with a review of that reminder of the darkest hour of Jewish history. But in between is the Preacher's key (verses 12–15):

Verse 12: Beware of having an evil, unbelieving <u>heart</u> (*kardia*, Strong's number 2588, "man's entire mental and moral activity, both the rational and the emotional elements" and "figuratively for the hidden springs of the personal life").

Verse 13: Encourage (*parakaleo*, Strong's number 3870, "call to one's side," "call to one's aid," "beseech" to produce a particular effect such as comfort, etc.) points to believers' responsibility to one another!

Verse 14: Hold fast the beginning of our assurance (*hupostasis*, Strong's number 5287, our "foundation in the person of Jesus." *** It is the same word used in 1:3, "nature"***).

Verse 15: Psalm 95:7—hear His voice (*shama*, Strong's number 8085, [9] "in the case of hearing and hearkening to a higher authority, *shama* refers to obey").

The Church's one foundation is Jesus Christ her Lord.
She is His new creation by water and the word.
From heaven He came and sought her to be His holy bride;
With His own blood He bought her, and for her life He died.

'Mid toil and tribulation, and tumult of her war,
she waits the consummation of peace forevermore;
Till with the vision glorious, her longing eyes are blest,
and the great church victorious shall be the church at rest!

Yet she on earth hath union with God the Three in One.
And mystic sweet communion with those whose rest is won;
O happy ones and holy! Lord, give us grace that we,
like them the meek and lowly, on high may dwell with Thee![27]

---

27   Samuel J. Stone, "The Church's One Foundation." 1866.

CHAPTER 4
The Rest of Faith

Things didn't seem right. Doubt was casting its shadow over the hearts and minds of the Preacher's audience. Weren't we, as all the early church, told that Jesus was returning to set up His kingdom? Not only this, but He was returning soon! Did we miss Him? Did we miss His "rest"? These feelings of doubt were common in the early church. The Apostle Paul addressed the same issue with the church in Thessalonica. Because they had forsaken the temple ritual, Jewish believers were often criticized for having no high priest.[28] In the history of the Jews, it was believed that if one followed the Laws of the Sabbath perfectly, God would be impressed and set up His kingdom on earth more quickly (i.e., the better our works, the sooner His kingdom would come to earth). Thus, personal works became more important. But we who believe confess by faith our relationship to God through Jesus Christ. Again, have we missed His rest?

---

28   Robert Gromacki, *Stand Bold in Grace* (Kress Christian Publications, 2002), page 81.

In the New Testament, we see two words used for rest. The first word, *anapauo*, is used by Jesus in Matthew 11:27. It is a word that means "refreshed" for the weary. Learning from Jesus as your rabbi, you'll find that His (yoke) interpretation of the law is easy and the burden to learn is light (Jesus states His yoke in Matthew 22:34–40 and affirms His yoke in Luke 10:25–28). The second word for rest is *katapausis*, to relax, enjoy tranquility, peacefulness. It is this term for rest that the Preacher uses in Hebrews. It was this rest that some of Hebrews may have seemed to miss. Not only this, but faith is the key to rest, and if they were losing faith, the Preacher was warning them they could lose out on God's rest!

The rest of which the Preacher is speaking may be called "the rest of faith,"[29] which is *present* and is a *spiritual* rest. This is in contrast to the millennial rest that the early church was anticipating and some felt they may have missed! The Preacher states in verse 3 that "we who are believing enter that rest." Please note that in the original language, this phrase is in present tense. We understand from the Preacher that *the rest of faith* "is not something simply to be hoped for in the future. It is an essential part of the present reality for Christians."[30] It is a "rest appropriated by faith and enjoyed even in the midst of the conflicts, obstacles, and oppositions of life. Such was the rest missed by the Exodus generation; and the rest entered into by Joshua's generation when by faith they possessed the land and enjoyed its blessings. We who believe enter this

29   Everett Harrison, ed., *The Wycliffe Bible Commentary* (Moody Press, 1962), page 1412.
30   Donald Guthrie, *Hebrews* (InterVarsity Press, 1983), page 40.

rest."[31] The Preacher highlighted the pattern of rest (*katapausis*) by using God at creation as an example. To show that this rest is continual (present), he quotes David from Psalm 95.

We first view the seventh day of creation, "and God rested from all His works." The analogy is that there were no more works; God rested from working. As so, we have stopped our works and have entered, by God's grace, into a spiritual rest (relationship) with God through Jesus Christ. We are saved by grace and not by works. When do we enter this rest? Why, *today* of course! The Preacher explains that this rest is not a one-and-done event. It happened when the Israelites entered the Promised Land, and generations later David writes to remind us not to harden our hearts. If this rest was done, completed, at the Exodus, then the Holy Spirit through David would not be writing about it in the present tense. The Preacher challenges his audience to not follow the example of disobedience of the disbelieving generation that was not allowed to enter the rest. The Preacher clearly feels there is a danger that there may be those who are guilty of the same sort of disobedience.

Israel was evangelized (had good news preached), and we who believe have been evangelized. We notice not only the activity but also the character of the *word* of God. We remember from lesson one: "Israel's hope, it is reasoned, cannot survive if it is detached from that which *God has communicated to her*." What is the character of the word of God?

---

31   J. Dwight Pentecost, *Faith That Endures* (Kregel Publications, 1992), page 83.

- Active
- Sharper than a two-edged sword (most feared weapon of that day)

The word of God judges intentions of the heart. Within the definition of intentions (*ennoia*) is the "seat of reflective consciousness" or the very basis of perception and understanding. There is not a morsel of thought that escapes God. The term of "laid bare" is the Greek word *gumnos*, meaning "naked," either absolutely or figuratively.[32]

Drawing near to God's throne is a new concept for Jews of the early church. Throughout their history, they knew the danger of coming near to a king's throne without an invitation (see the book of Esther). Only after proper confession and sacrifice could the High Priest (and the High Priest *only*) enter the Holy of Holies where the "mercy seat" was placed on which God was present.

In his book, *The Tabernacle: Shadows of the Messiah*, David M. Levy describes the High Priest functioning at the mercy seat while the congregation waited outside the tabernacle for the High Priest to appear. "First, the High Priest offered a bullock as a sin offering for himself and his house before he made an offering for the nation of Israel. Next, he took a censer full of burning coals from the brazen alter, put two handfuls of sweet incense into a golden bowl, and entered the Holy of Holies. He poured the incense on the coals, which emitted

---

32   James Strong, *The New Strong's Expanded Dictionary of Bible Words* (Nelson Publishers, 2001), pages 1257 and 1030.

a thick, fragrant, cloudy smoke that filled the chamber. The cloud of smoke twisting upward represented the prayers of God's people, offered as protection, on this holiest of days (Day of Atonement).

"The High Priest returned to the brazen altar, took a basin full of the bullock's blood, and again entered the Holy of Holies to sprinkle the blood on the mercy seat. Dipping his finger into the basin of blood, he sprinkled the mercy seat seven times. The blood made it possible for God to show mercy to the nation of Israel. Sprinkling the blood seven times spoke of the completed atonement.

"The High Priest chose two goats of equal color, size, and value from the congregation of Israel. Lots were cast by the High Priest to determine which of the two goats was to be slain." The goat that wasn't slain was used as the "scapegoat."

"The High Priest then offered the first goat as a sin offering. Its blood was sprinkled several times in the tabernacle. First, it was sprinkled before the mercy seat in the Holy of Holies in the same manner as the blood of the bullock. Second, he sprinkled the horns of the altar of incense seven times to cleanse it from the contamination of Israel. Third, he went to the brazen altar and mixed the blood of the bullock and the blood of the goat into one basin. Dipping his finger into the basin of blood, he sprinkled the horns of the brazen altar seven times, cleansing it from the uncleanness of Israel.

"The congregation of Israel patiently and prayerfully waited outside of the tabernacle for the High Priest to appear before them. Naturally, many questions passed through their minds: Would God accept the blood offered by the High Priest? If God did not accept the blood offering, would He slay the High Priest in the Holy of Holies? Would God be merciful to Israel or would He bring judgment?"[33] The High Priest would come out at the gate of the tabernacle with his hands raised, symbolizing that God had accepted their sacrifice.

It should be noted that there is no "throne of grace" within the Jewish sacrificial system.[34] The Preacher makes an effort to reveal that since Jesus is now our High Priest, He is able to sympathize with us who are tempted because He finished His redemptive work and sat down beside the heavenly throne. That throne has become a place where grace reigns and is dispensed[35]; we approach the throne confident that we will find mercy and grace in our time of need.

Thus, we (Hebrew Christians) have a high priest who was tempted as we are tempted, and He can sympathize with our needs. God's throne is a throne of grace and not judgment! We, by faith, enter into God's rest today. Despite conflicts and unrest, trials, temptations, and persecution, today if you hear His voice, do not harden your hearts!

---

33   David M. Levy, *The Tabernacle: Shadows of the Messiah* (The Friends of Israel Gospel Ministry, Inc., 1993), pages 90–91.

34   Robert Gromacki, *Stand Bold in Grace* (Kress Christian Publications, 2002), page 84.

35   Ibid.

CHAPTER 5
Jesus the Superior High Priest

As we begin chapter 5, the Preacher is continuing his defense of Jesus as the Great High Priest. Finishing chapter 4, we today would most likely say that the Preacher has made his point. Jesus is the Great High Priest, superior to any past high priest. But evidently the Preacher feels the need to expound on the subject. After all, his audience was comprised of "traitors to the faith" and, thus, was now without a high priest. Not only this, but we recall that one of the reasons Hebrew Christians were wavering in their faith was because they remembered what they were told (or possibly what they had seen) of the Crucifixion. Jesus could save others, but He couldn't save himself! This weak and rejected man who was cursed and placed to die on a cross is not even from the tribe of Levi, but now is not just a high priest but the Great High Priest. "Faith comes from what is heard," and that is why the congregation must "hold fast to our confession" (4:14) and "pay greater attention to what we have heard" (2:1). The Preacher must use words to reinforce the truth that Jesus is, indeed, the Great High Priest.[36] The Preacher at this point goes through the high priest qualifications as though he has interviewed Jesus for the job and is now recommending Him for employment.

1. Function of the High Priest
    a. Verse 1: The High Priest is as human as the next person. He takes the gifts and sacrifices of the people and offers them to God on their behalf. He is the mediator between God and humans.
    b. Verses 9–10: Jesus, as High Priest, is greater than the ancient high priests for at least two reasons:
        i. He Himself is the source of salvation.
        ii. The old priesthood had to go back time and again to the altar (another year, new sins and new sacrifices) while Jesus offered Himself for atonement of sins "once and for all" (see chapter 9).

2. Person of the High Priest
    a. Verses 2–3: The ancient high priests had their own weaknesses and failings just as those whom they represented to God. Being every bit as sinful, they offered sacrifices for their own sins as well as the sins of others. Being like others, they could sympathize with others in their human experiences.
    b. Verses 7–8: The Preacher uses graphic words (loud cries and tears; also see Psalm 22) to show Jesus's

---

36 Thomas G. Long, *Hebrews: Interpretations* (Westminster John Knox Press, 1997), page 66.

human condition and ability to sympathize with those He represented before His Father. The point the Preacher is making is that unlike the old priesthood, Jesus was fully human, but in His humanity He never sinned.

3. Appointment of High Priest
    a. Verses 4–6, verses 8–10
        i. Old priesthood was appointed by God, from tribe of Levi, for his lifetime.
        ii. Jesus was appointed by God as a Priest *forever*. Not only this, but He was appointed to *Sonship* (Psalm 2:7). And again, not only this, but He was appointed High Priest in the *order of Melchizedek* (Psalm 110:4).

At this point, the Preacher wants to say more about Melchizedek (verses 11–14). One could think that he had substantially made his point, but priestly appointment "in the order of Melchizedek" must have been new to his audience, at least inasmuch as being appointed to the high priest position allows. But why can't he continue his explanation?

"The rebuke in this passage seems to include all the Preacher's listeners, that these believers had made no progress either doctrinally or experimentally, that they did not understand Melchizedek, and furthermore, what they should have known, they did not."[37] The Preacher uses terms:[38]

---

37   Everett Harrison, ed., *The Wycliffe Bible Commentary* (Moody Press, 1962), page 1414.
38   A. T. Robertson, *Word Pictures of the New Testament*, *Volume 5* (Broadman Press, 1932), pages 371–372.

- Dull of hearing (*nothroi tais akoais*)—slow and sluggish in the mind as well as in the ears (*nothroi*, can also mean "stupid").
- Babe (*nepios*)—"suckling," only able to take milk.
- Mature, who because of practice (*gegymnasmena*); they were as "fully trained athletes," ready for the contest because of their discipline and training; "by reason of use one gains such skill."[39]

---

39   Ibid.

CHAPTER 6
Forward to Maturity

This chapter begins with the Preacher leading his audience to move forward "to the goal set for us by God" (verse 1). That is the meaning of the word "maturity" (*teliotes*, meaning "goal"or "purpose"). The Preacher doesn't want to repeat the foundations of salvation. "Going back to the foundations will not help those who have *deliberately turned away* from God."[40] Let's move forward to maturity.

There have been those who did not move forward toward maturity, who turned away from God. They knew the foundations of salvation. These persons were enlightened in that they received and accepted the saving grace of God through Jesus's death and resurrection. They understood salvation by grace and not works, or in keeping the law. The terms the Preacher uses show that these people were knowledgeable and participated even in miracles. It is not specifically clear that the

---

40   J. B. Phillips, *The New Testament in Modern English* (Galahad Books , 1958), page 461.

Preacher was speaking of individuals in his audience, but some believers (at least in general) had "fallen away" (*parapipto*), that is "apostatized," a *willing reversal* to the adherence to the realities and facts of the faith.[41] The Preacher is trying to make his point; it was the Preacher's "purpose to portray extreme peril so that those tempted to apostasy might have the strongest possible example."[42] I'm reminded of the words the Apostle Paul used as he encouraged his readers in his letter to the church in Galatia: "you stupid Galatians," "oh, you dear idiots of Galatia," "you foolish Galatians," etc. (Galatians 3:1, from different versions/translations). One does not use gentle terms when dealing with apostasy!

The Preacher illustrates his message (verses 5 and 6) by using a picture of people who "when they first trusted Jesus, they thereby acknowledged that His crucifixion had been unjust and a result of man's sinful rejection of the Savior. But by renouncing this opinion (apostasy), they reaffirmed the view of Jesus's enemies that He deserved to die on a cross. In this sense, they were crucifying the Son of God all over again!"[43] Donald Gutherie states, "The intention is clearly not to give a dissertation on the nature of grace (*can one lose his salvation?*), but to give a warning in the strongest possible terms."[44] (Italics are mine.)

---

41 James Strong, *The New Strong's Expanded Dictionary of Bible Words* (Nelson Publishers, 2001), page 1293.

42 Everett Harrison, ed., *The Wycliffe Bible Commentary* (Moody Press, 1962), page 1415.

43 *The Bible Knowledge Commentary, an Exposition of the Scriptures by Dallas Seminary Faculty* (SP Publications, Inc., 1983), page 795.

44 Donald Guthrie, *Hebrews* (InterVarsity Press, 1983), page 148.

In verses 7 and 8, the Preacher uses an illustration in which "thorns and thistles" are the result of disobedience (Genesis 3:17–18). It is also possible that the Preacher had in mind the land of the Jordan valley (Genesis 13:10), which was "well watered like the garden of the Lord" but was subsequently judged (Sodom and Gomorrah) by God and destroyed by fire.

The land with thorns and thistles is "worthless" (*adokimos*); this word shows that the land was not arbitrarily seen as worthless and thus burned. The word is a picture of one examining the land, as one examined the first land and found fruit. The second was also examined, but no fruit was found, only thorns and thistles. Thus it was burned as there was no presence of effective fruit. But even though the Preacher is using such negative terms and descriptions (verse 9), he is confident the "beloved" will move toward maturity and use God's blessings to produce good fruit. "Even though it might seem that he is addressing them as unbelievers, he is sure of their salvation and is confident that their salvation will produce good fruit. The good fruit he has already seen in the work and labor of love that they have carried on in Christ's name."[45]

The reason for his confidence in his audience is because in His covenant with Abraham, God swore by Himself! While they believed God's promises, the people were finding it difficult to be patient. So the Preacher uses Abraham as an example of patience.

The Preacher's example is based on the oral customs of

---

45   J. Dwight Pentecost, *Faith That Endures* (Kregel Publications, 1992), page 109.

swearing or oath taking in the ancient world to guarantee trustworthiness of one's words. An oath is an appeal to God as a witness on some disputed matter. If trust was in question, then a party in an agreement could raise the stakes and swear a divine oath—basically saying that if he was lying, may he be struck down by God! Abraham believed God's promise, but he did ask of God, "How may I know that I shall possess it (the land)?" (Genesis 15:8) Abraham wanted a sign "for his patient endurance while he was waiting for the fulfillment of the promise."[46] Having no one greater to swear by, and to show that the covenant was dependent upon God alone, Abraham was rendered incapable of participating in the ritual. Abraham's faith then rested on two things: the promise of God and the oath of God, which are immutable, absolute. God cannot lie!

So where does this leave the Preacher's audience? Their (our) hope is:

1. It is an anchor.
    a. Sure (*asphale*) and indestructible
    b. Steadfast (*bebaian*), having no innate weaknesses
    c. One enters within the veil, in the presence of God, a place formerly for the High Priest.

2. It is Jesus Christ!
    a. Forerunner (*prodromos*) is the term used of soldiers who were sent in advance of a marching army.

---

46   J. Dwight Pentecost, *Faith That Endures* (Kregel Publications, 1992), page 112.

No high priest within Israel was a "forerunner," as no Israelite could follow him into the Holy of Holies. But Jesus "has entered into that area, in the very presence of God as our Representative, and His presence there is a pledge that we shall soon follow."[47]

---

47   H. A. Ironside, *Hebrews* (Kregel Publications, 1932), pages 66–67.

CHAPTER 7
Order of Melchizedek

We start this chapter with a bit of history. Certainly discussing anything about Abraham (Abram) will be history. The historical background of the first reference to Melchizedek in scripture is important. Lot, Abraham's nephew, had separated from Abraham and settled in Sodom. The Elamites formed a coalition under Chedorlaomer and successfully invaded Sodom and Gomorrah. Lot was taken captive. Abraham felt responsible to deliver his nephew from his captors, so he organized 318 shepherds into an army.

Land that had been given to Abraham by the blood covenant had been taken from the rightful heirs. It was Abraham's faith in this covenant that was the basis on which he was determined to retake the land. Not only this, but Lot was also present at the time when "Abram called upon the name of the Lord" (Genesis 13:1–5), and thus Abraham believed that Lot was a son of the promise. God responded to Abraham's faith and gave him a great victory.[48] Abraham returned from battle with the spoils of victory; it was God's victory through Abraham.

We digress a bit before we look at Melchizedek to review the position of priest. The Aaronic priesthood would not begin for some four hundred years in the future at this point in time. We see in scripture that God had appointed mediators between Himself and the people prior to the Exodus. For example, we see in Job 1:5 that Job acted in this role. We are told that "when the days of the feast had run their course, Job would send and consecrate them, and he would rise early in the morning and offer burnt offerings according to the number of them all. For Job said, 'It may be that my children have sinned, and cursed God in their hearts.' Thus Job did continually." So we realize that a priest prior to Aaron was not uncommon. But we learn that Melchizedek's priesthood was uncommon.

Melchizedek is mentioned in only three passages of scripture: Hebrews 5:5 through 7:28, Genesis 14:17–24, and Psalm 110:4. He has two significant titles. First, he was the King of Salem, and second, he was a "priest of God Most High." The Preacher tells us (verse 2) that the translation of his name means "king of righteousness" and "king of peace." Scripture has neither mention of his genealogy nor of his death. By the silence of his birth and death, one sees no end to his priesthood as one would with the Levitical priests. In this manner, he is "made like the Son of God" (verse 3). It is by these qualities—righteousness, peace, and timelessness—which point

---

48   J. Dwight Pentecost, *Faith That Endures* (Kregel Publications, 1992), page 115.

forward to Jesus, the Great High Priest.[49] It is these qualities that make up the *"order* of Melchizedek."

Melchizedek meets Abraham. It is not Abraham's victory or his faith that the Preacher wants to highlight to his audience; it is the blessing of Melchizedek, *placing him superior to Abraham,* the patriarch. This is his focus for which there is "no dispute" (verse 7). One who receives tithes is greater than the one presenting the tithes (see verse 4). Melchizedek was blessing Abraham and receiving tithes from Abraham (the patriarch). "What does all this mean spiritually? Observe (*theoreite,* or contemplate) the greatness of the one whom Abraham acknowledged to be superior by giving him tithes. The important truth is that the priesthood of Melchizedek was greater than the priesthood of Aaron and the Levites because (figuratively) the latter priesthood offered tithes to God through the earlier priesthood in the person of Abraham."[50] Along with this manner of speaking, the Levitical priesthood also was blessed by Melchizedek. This first comparison the Preacher is making then is that Melchizedek's priesthood is greater than the Levitical priesthood. "It is the two orders of priesthood that he has in mind."[51]

Numbers 18:26f sets out the rights of the Levitical priests to command tithes from the people. Melchizedek received tithes from the patriarch without command for them. The

---

49   Thomas G. Long, *Hebrews: Interpretation* (Westminster John Knox Press, 1997), page 85.
50   5Everett Harrison, ed., *The Wycliffe Bible Commentary* (Moody Press, 1962), page 1416.
51   Donald Guthrie, *Hebrews* (InterVarsity Press, 1983), page 161.

words used for Melchizedek receiving tithes are in the present tense showing the *continuance* of this order of priesthood. The Preacher is transporting the event to the readers' present time.

So we can see that the Preacher, by setting up his point (by use of the old priesthood) that Melchizedek is greater than Abraham (and thus the Levitical priesthood), will move on to show that Jesus is the Great High Priest in the order of Melchizedek, and that His priesthood is far better and eternal.

In verse 11, the Preacher mentions "perfection" (*teleiosis*), which is a word picture of a completion, an end accomplishment as the effect of a process.[52] We are "human" (fallible), imperfect, yet approach a perfect and holy God. "The conditional sentence (verse 11) *if perfection had been attainable...what further need...* depends on two assumptions. It assumes that 'perfection' is *the* desirable end, and it also assumes that the Levitical priesthood and with it the law could not produce such perfection."[53] So there, naturally, was the need for a high priest in the order of Melchizedek and not in the order of Aaron. When the priesthood (verse 12) is changed, it necessitates a change in the law. We see in verse 19 there is a better (*kreitton*) hope, that is, a more powerful and effective hope through which we can approach a perfect and holy God. In his letter to the Romans, Paul states basically that the law only shows our imperfection (Romans 7:4–11). We have a better hope!

---

52 James Strong, *The New Strong's Expanded Dictionary of Bible Words* (Nelson Publishers, 2001), page 1409.
53 Donald Guthrie, *Hebrews* (InterVarsity Press, 1983), page 163.

The order of Melchizedek (righteous, peace, and timeless) is better than the *order* of Aaron (through Levi, continual sacrifices, lifetime limited, etc.). Jesus Christ is superior to any order. Why? First, because, as David writes, "the Lord (God the Father) has sworn and will not change His mind" in telling my Lord (Jesus the Son) that "You are a priest forever according to the order of Melchizedek" (Psalm 110:4). Besides a timeless priesthood ("forever"), what can we understand or appreciate in regard to this new priesthood when compared to the old? We first remember that, at this point in his message, this information is not exclusive from what the Preacher has already stated. Who is Jesus? We look back to chapter 1 of our study to remind ourselves:

He is no "supermonarch" but God incarnate! Focus on the greatness of our Lord and Savior. This revelation through the Son is not viewed by the Preacher as simply another progressive form of revelation (i.e., another revelation through the communication form of a prophet). It is God's ultimate and climactic revelation of Himself through the Son[54] or "through Son."

1. Whom God appointed heir of all things ("appointment" signifying authority)
2. Through whom He made the worlds ("He ordered the ages" of time from eternity past through eternity)
3. Who is the brightness of His glory (not a reflection but an original, "is" signifying unbroken fellowship with the Father)

---

54   J. Dwight Pentecost, *Faith That Endures* (Kregel Publications, 1992), page 45.

4. The express image of His person (all that is in the Father is in the Son)

5. He upholds all things by the word of His power. The word "upholding" has in it the idea of carrying something along to a designated end. Not only is the Son the One who was the architect of the ages, He is also the One who through the ages has been carrying creation to its designated end—by "power," implying "authoritative command that is consequently executed."[55]

6. He had Himself purged our sins and

7. Sat down at the right hand of the Majesty, which implies taking a seat of honor and authority at the completion (perfection) of a specified work.

Keeping in mind all that the Preacher has presented to us about Jesus Christ, we see in Jesus as the Great High Priest first a better hope in that Jesus brings us to perfection; stated another way, Jesus presents us to His Father as perfect! The Father sees us in Jesus, thus He sees us as perfection *forever*! The former ineffective regulations and commands for sacrifices (that could never bring perfection) presented by a high priest who himself is a sinner is now replaced by an *order* of righteousness and peace (*eirene*, legal term for one who is acquitted of his sin even though he indeed sinned) forever, by One who is sinless!

---

55   Ibid, page 48.

Jesus, My Great High Priest

Jesus, my great High Priest, offered His blood and died;
My guilty conscience seeks no sacrifice beside.
His powerful blood did once atone, and now it pleads be-
fore the throne.

To this dear Surety's hand will I commit my cause;
He answers and fulfills His Father's broken laws.
Behold my soul at freedom set; my Surety paid the dreadful
debt.

My Advocate appears for my defense on high;
The Father bows His ears and lays His thunder by.
Not all that hell or sin can say shall turn His heart, His love,
away.

Should all the hosts of death and powers of hell unknown
Put their most dreadful forms of rage and mischief on,
I shall be safe, for Christ displays His conquering power and
guardian grace!

Isaac Watts (1674–1748)

Amen!

CHAPTER 8
Better Covenant

We start our examination of Hebrews chapter 8 with some Old Testament prophecies. Although this passage is not used by the Preacher, it is from Zechariah 6:11–13. Tell Joshua, son of Jehozadak, "This is what the Lord Almighty says: 'Here is the man whose name is the Branch, and he will branch out from His place and build the temple of the Lord. It is He who will build the temple of the Lord, and He will be clothed with majesty and will sit and rule on His throne. And He will be Priest on His throne. And there will be harmony between the two.'"

Psalm 110:1–2, 4: "The Lord says to my Lord, 'Sit at My right hand, until I make Your enemies a footstool for Your feet.' The Lord will stretch forth Your strong scepter from Zion, saying 'rule in the midst of Your enemies.' The Lord has sworn and will not change His mind. 'You are priest forever according to the order of Melchizedek.'" As prophesied, Jesus is sitting on the throne in majesty as Ruler to come, because the Lord will give dominion to the King (our Lord). Not only this, but Jesus will also be King *and* Priest (remember the order of Melchizedek: he was king and priest). Jesus will perform these two functions in harmony.

Without getting into eschatology (e.g., Jesus is not king yet), our focus is in regard to the present posture of Jesus. "The posture of sitting at the right hand of the throne of God connotes both royal and priestly aspects. Here the author is bringing together Psalm 110:1 and 4 at a critical juncture in his theological development. Similar statements have already been made in Hebrews 1:3 and 13. That Christ, as the priest/king, is "seated" further separates the person and work of Christ from the Levitical priesthood in that no high priest ever performed priestly duties while seated. There was no chair in the Holy of Holies. Furthermore, Hebrews 10: 11–14 stresses that every priest "stands" daily, making the required sacrifices that "can never take away sins." Jesus, however, "having offered one sacrifice for sins for all time, *sat down at the right hand of God.* The finality of Jesus's sacrifice is observed in his seated posture at the right hand."[56] This point is made for the purpose of establishing that Christ as the superior High Priest is not on earth but in heaven.[57] He is ministering in the sanctuary of the "true tent" created by God and not man. On Sinai, Moses received instructions for the earthly tabernacle, which is only a copy (shadow) of the heavenly tabernacle.

The Preacher has made clear two attributes that make Jesus a

---

56   David L. Allen, *Hebrews, The New American Commentary* (B & H Publishing Group, 2010), page 440.

57   Ibid, page 441.

superior high priest: position in heaven (4:14–16) and a better order (chapter 7). Three more are coming:

1. Better covenant (chapter 8)
2. Better sanctuary (chapter 9:1–11)
3. Better sacrifice (chapter 9:12 through 10:18)

We begin now with verse 7: "If the first covenant had been faultless there would be no need for a second." This first covenant can be found beginning in Exodus 20:22 ("Then the Lord said to Moses...") and ending in Exodus 23:33, with the people's affirmation in Exodus 24:3: "All the words which the Lord has spoken we will do!" The first covenant included such laws for

- General form of worship (20:22–26)
- Civil and social relations (21:1 through 23:13)
- Laws regarding property (21:33 through 22:17)
- Moral and religious laws (22:18 through 23: 9)
- Humanitarian laws (22:21–27)
- Reviling God or the ruler (22:28)
- Upholding truth and justice (23:1–9)
- A church calendar (23:10–13)
- Three rules to observe in the feasts (23:18–19)
- Conclusion (23:20–33)[58]

But this covenant failed as the people sinned and did not hold their part of the covenant.

---

58   Everett Harrison, ed., *The Wycliffe Bible Commentary* (Moody Press, 1962), pages 68–73.

Jesus is now a superior high priest, and His ministry, according to the Preacher, is that He is (verse 6, New American Standard Bible) "mediator of a better (*kreitton*, denotes power in activity and effect) covenant (*diatheke*, a contract), which has been enacted on better promises (*epaggelia*, pledge, a divine assurance of good)." But God's promises are equally pure, we may counter. "It is preferable to take 'better' to refer to the higher spiritual purpose inherent in the new covenant, e.g., the idea of the law written on the heart (verse 10). Promises that can do that must be better than promises which could only lead to the codification of the old law (i.e., the Law of Moses)."[59]

Any covenant with God is inevitably one sided, favoring God. Man is fallible by definition, so nature requires the Mediator to act on man's behalf before God to keep us in fellowship with God. Indeed He does act on God's behalf before man, but a defecting God or the Law of Moses is not or was not the problem. The law "being faulty" does not point to its inability but to man's experience under the law that was faulty. The problem was more with the people than with the covenant.[60] "The law was our disciplinarian until Christ came" (Galatians 3: 24). The law showed our sinfulness. So with a better covenant, God meets us where we are as the new covenant has the remedy for sin.

J. B. Phillips interprets verse 8 just prior to quoting Jeremiah: "actually, however, God does show Himself dissatisfied for He

---

59   Donald Guthrie, *Hebrews* (InterVarsity Press, 1983), page 177.
60   David L. Allen, *Hebrews, The New American Commentary* (B & H Publishing Group, 2010), page 445.

says..."[61] The Preacher quotes Jeremiah's (31:31–34) prophecy of the new covenant ("new" Hebrew *hadas,* Greek *kainos;* renewed, restoration of character or nature). This is the longest Old Testament quote found in the New Testament. "God initiated the Mosaic covenant knowing full well it would be ineffective in dealing with the sin problem. The Mosaic covenant was 'anticipatory' of the new covenant in the sense that God had always planned for the new covenant. The first covenant did not 'fail' but was rather insufficient by design. In this sense the old covenant fulfilled its God-given purpose."[62] (Jesus mentions this new covenant in Luke 22:20 as does Paul in II Corinthians 3:6.)

The new covenant is superior because

- Of one's inner inclination to obey God (laws in minds and hearts)
- Of one's firm relationship with God (I will be their God; they will be My people.)
- Of one's knowledge of God (They will know Me.)
- Of one's being forgiven of his or her sins (I will remember their sins no more.)

In the last verse of this chapter, the Preacher notes that when the Lord introduced the new covenant, the old covenant became obsolete (*palaioo,* worn out, opposite of *kainos*). "*Whatever* is becoming obsolete and growing old is ready to

---

61   J. B. Phillips, *The New Testament in Modern English* (Galahad Books, 1958), page 465.
62   Barry Joslin, *Hebrews, Christ, and the Law: The Theology of the Mosaic Law in Hebrews* (Paternoster, 2008), page 229.

disappear." To what is the word "whatever" referring? At the time this was communicated, prior to AD 70, sacrificial offerings were still being made in the temple by the High Priest. These ceremonies were spiritually outdated, worn out. The Preacher's words suggest that he is referring to the prophecy that the temple will be destroyed (Matthew 24:1–2, Luke 19:41–44). Thus, the present sacrifices are obsolete, and the place where such sacrifices are made is ready to disappear without one stone being left on another.

We go back to chapter 1:1–2 and remember that "God, after He spoke long ago to the fathers in the prophets in many portions and in many ways, in these last days has spoken to us in (His) Son." As stated previously in our study, in the original language of verse 2, there is "no article or pronoun here with the preposition, giving the absolute sense of 'Son.' Here the idea is not merely what Jesus said but what He is, God's Son who reveals the Father.[63] Thus, "God spoke to us through Son!" The Preacher continues in 1:3, "and He (Jesus) is the radiance of His (God the Father) glory…" At this point, it's like we've come full circle: the Preacher was telling us about the new covenant at the very beginning of his sermon. Why the new covenant is superior can be seen in the very beginning verses of Hebrews.

---

63   Dr. A. T. Robertson, *Word Pictures of the New Testament, Volume 5* (Broadman Press, 1932), page 335.

CHAPTER 9
Better Sanctuary

As we continue our study, let's remind ourselves that "it is important to keep the rhetorical situation of Hebrews in mind. The original readers (or listeners) were not students in a class on world religions debating the relative merits of Judaism versus Christianity. They were disheartened members of a Christian community who had begun to lose their grip on their own beliefs and commitments."[64]

The Preacher continues his efforts to make clear the attributes that show Jesus a superior high priest (position in heaven, 4:14–16; a better order, chapter 7; and a better covenant, chapter 8). He continues now with his exposition on the better sanctuary, noting the tabernacle rather than the temple. The Preacher begins with a view of the old sanctuary, continues with the priestly activity, and follows up with the greater and perfect sanctuary and the actions of the new high priest.

---

64   Thomas G. Long, *Hebrews: Interpretation* (Westminster John Knox Press, 1997), page 12.

The view of the old sanctuary is rather brief, and before any-one can get nostalgic for the good old days, the Preacher will announce the presentation is over: "but of these things we cannot now speak in detail" (verse 5). I remember visiting with my wife's great uncle late in his years. We were looking at pictures of the family, and though his memory was fading, he would smile and point at pictures of himself and others when they were young. As a picture of his mother was pre-sented to him, his eyes welled up with tears and a slight smile came across his face, and all he could say was "ohhhhh!" as he kissed the picture. He held it tightly and would touch the photographed face of one he obviously loved and missed. It was as though he couldn't get enough of the view of his mother, who had passed long ago.

The Preacher knew his audience. They were longing for sta-bility, something familiar, something that made them feel as though there was a place for them in their present culture and environment. To lead them to his point of Jesus being in a greater sanctuary, he couldn't dwell on the old sanctuary for long. "The Preacher is playing peekaboo with the congrega-tion; alert to the fact the one glance inside the Holy of Holies will only whet their appetite for more."[65] And so the Preacher just allows a quick gaze at the sanctuary.

The first covenant was inseparably joined to the Levitical sac-rificial system, which had to function in the appointed place, namely the "worldly sanctuary." The adjective "worldly" (kos-mikon) refers to the geographical location of the building, not

---

65   Ibid, page 94.

to an ethical weakness:[66] worldly as in contrast with heavenly. The Preacher lays out the tabernacle that was inside the courtyard. There were two sections that comprised the tabernacle: the outer area, called the Holy Place, was separated by a veil from the inner area, called the Holy of Holies. The furnishings of these areas included a lampstand and the table of showbread, and just before the veil that separates the Holy Place from the Holy of Holies is the altar of incense. In the Holy of Holies is the Ark of the Covenant, which held a golden jar of manna, Aaron's rod that had budded signifying the priesthood would come from the tribe of Levi (Aaron's tribe), and the tablets of the Ten Commandments. The Ark was covered on all sides with gold. On the top of the Ark were cherubim facing the mercy seat where the Shekinah Glory of God rested.

"In Hebrews 9:3–4 the altar of incense is considered part of the most holy place; apparently this was because on the Day of Atonement the high priest took incense from this altar into the most holy place (Leviticus 16:12–13)."[67] We need to note that according to God's instructions to Moses in Leviticus, the only piece of furniture in the Holy of Holies was the Ark of the Covenant. We know, too, that burning incense was a daily task performed by the priests along with caring for the lampstand and table of showbread. Since only the High Priest could enter the Holy of Holies on the Day of Atonement, the altar of incense had to be located in the Holy Place accessible to the priests.

---

66   Robert Gromacki, *Stand Bold in Grace* (Kress Christian Publications, 2002), page 144.
67   *The Bible Knowledge Commentary, An Exposition of the Scriptures by Dallas Seminary Faculty* (Victor Books, 1985), page 154.

So we have, Hebrew Christians, priests continually entering the Holy Place performing daily tasks and rituals but only the High Priest entering the Holy of Holies one time a year *with blood of animals* for his sins and the sins of the people. These are sins that were committed unwittingly. These arrangements (or regulations) and furnishings here in the earthly sanctuary stood as symbols until Jesus Christ came.

To help give authority to his words, the Preacher brings in the Holy Spirit as if to remind his audience of the indwelling presence now within them (they are now seeing "spiritually"). The Holy Spirit is showing that while the work in the earthly outer sanctuary is still being performed, there is no direct access to God for them since they don't enter the Holy of Holies. Gifts and sacrifices cannot make one perfect in God's sight. What's more, these regulations were for the body (verse 10, *sarx*[68]) and not involving the spirit.

We remember from the Preacher's previous words leading to this section of the better sanctuary that the new covenant is superior because

- Of one's inner inclination to obey God (laws in minds and hearts)
- Of one's firm relationship with God (I will be their God; they will be My people.)
- Of one's knowledge of God (They will know Me.)
- Of one's being forgiven of their sins (I will remember their sins no more.)

---

68   James Strong, *The New Strong's Expanded Dictionary of Bible Words* (Nelson Publishers, 2001), page 1360._

Our relationship with God is spiritual!

So, with this in mind, we come to the understanding that Jesus Christ the High Priest entered the perfect heavenly tabernacle, one not made with human hands. He didn't enter with the blood of animals but with His own blood once for all (not annually over and over again as the earthly High Priest). If the blood of animals could make the body pure, then how much more does the blood of Jesus Christ through the Spirit (*pneuma*[69]) purify our spirit (*suneidesis*,[70] the faculty by which we apprehend the will of God) so that we may serve the living God?

The mentioning of death in verse 15 is the segue the Preacher uses to state his comparison of purification through death (old covenant), verses 16–22, with purification through the death of Jesus Christ (new covenant), verses 23–28. First we see that the Preacher is using *diatheke*, the word for "covenant," to refer to a person's last will and testament. One's will is only valid when that person has died and never in force while that one is still living. Making the point of how death is associated with *diatheke* (will, covenant, and contract), there must be death for the covenant to be in effect.

Without the shedding of blood, there can be no remission of sin (verse 22). With the first covenant, the blood of animals was used. Animal sacrifices were involuntary, and on the Day of Atonement, this blood sacrifice did not pay the sin debt

---

69   Ibid, page 1321.
70   Ibid, page 1393.

but "only forestalled collection (of the indebtedness of sin) for another year."[71] But that sacrifice performed by Jesus in the heavenly sanctuary completely pays the sin debt. We remember Paul's words to the Romans in Romans 3:25, where he says, "A man who has faith is now freely acquitted in the eyes of God by His generous dealing in the redemptive act of Christ Jesus. God has appointed Him as the means of propitiation, a propitiation accomplished by the shedding of His blood, to be received and made effective in ourselves by faith."[72]

Jesus Christ has paid the debt of our sin, and when He returns, it will not be for the work of propitiation but to bring all who have received His salvation (spiritually and by faith) to the promised eternal inheritance!

---

71   J. Dwight Pentecost, *Faith that Endures* (Kregel Publications, 1992), page 147.
72   J. B. Phillips, *The New Testament in Modern English* (Galahad Books, 1958), Romans 3:25. Page 467

CHAPTER 10
Better Sacrifice

"They hoped against hope for the conversion of their people. When that hope vanished more and more, when some of their teachers had suffered martyrdom (13:7), when James, their revered leader, was stoned by the Jews (AD 62), and when the patriotic movement for the deliverance of Palestine from the hated yoke of the heathen Romans rose higher and higher, till it burst out at last in open rebellion (AD 66), it was very natural that those timid Christians should feel strongly tempted to apostatize from the poor, persecuted sect to the national religion, which they at heart still believed to be the best part of Christianity. The solemn services of the Temple, the ritual pomp and splendor of the Aaronic priesthood, the daily sacrifices, and all the sacred associations of the past had still a great charm for them, and allured them to their embrace. The danger was very strong and the warning of the Epistle fearfully solemn."[73]

---

73 Philip Schaff, *History of the Christian Church, Volume 1* (Hendrickson Publishers, Inc., 3rd printing, 2006), page 815.

We have come to the climax of the Preacher's sermon-within-a-sermon that began with chapter 7. He has stated his cases for the new covenant being superior to the old covenant, and for Jesus as High Priest being superior to the Levitical priests; Jesus's sacrifice is superior to animal sacrifices, and Jesus is now in the superior heavenly tabernacle. And now his message brings his audience to a high point: in Jesus Christ your sins are forgiven! You are made perfect! In regard to the Son's offering as being superior, it was made just one time, which was sufficient for the permanent cleansing of God's people.[74]

Again the Preacher points us to the law and sacrifices. If the sacrifices could make one perfect, if they could cleanse sin and not merely cover sin, then why were sacrifices continually necessary? The sacrificial system is nothing more than a reminder of sin. "In fact, the whole Day of Atonement ritual, repeated annually, is like a sledgehammer to the human spirit, pounding away year after year after year with its constant battering away on the theme of sin. In other words, it does not work to heal; it works only to drub it into us that we are sinful, sinful, sinful—guilty and unacceptable to God."[75] We are constantly mindful of guilt (a "consciousness of sin").

The Preacher quotes Psalm 40:6–8 from the Septuagint (LXX). We note in the first part that God ultimately is not satisfied with sacrifices as an end to guilt. We remember that the sacrifices on the Day of Atonement are made for sins performed

---

74   George H. Guthrie, , *Zondervan Illustrated Bible Backgrounds Commentary, Volume 4* (Zondervan Press, 2002), page 60.

75   Thomas G. Long, *Hebrews: Interpretation* (Westminster John Knox Press, 1997), page 101.

unintentionally. Guilt offerings are made individually for sins committed intentionally. These sacrifices are, again, made over and over. Thus, they cannot take away one's guilty feeling but only remind us that we are sinful. We are *oppressed by this consciousness of sin*, not free to have a personal relationship with God. The Preacher interprets the Psalm Christologically. The first part alludes to the sacrificial system of the old covenant, and Christ follows with "Then I said, 'Here I am. I have come to do Your will.'"

The Preacher uses legal terminology to describe Christ's willing submission. We note in verse 9, "He takes away the first" (*anairei to proton*) that "He may establish the second" (*hina to deuteron stesei*).[76] These are terms meaning "annulment" and "institution." The old covenant is no longer valid, and the new covenant is now established. We remember from Hebrews 8 that "God initiated the Mosaic covenant knowing full well it would be ineffective in dealing with the sin problem. The Mosaic covenant was 'anticipatory' of the new covenant in the sense that God had always planned for the new covenant. The first covenant did not 'fail' but was rather insufficient by design. In this sense the old covenant fulfilled its God-given purpose."[77] (Jesus mentions this new covenant in Luke 22:20 as does Paul in II Corinthians 3:6.)

The new covenant is superior because

---

76 A. T. Robertson, *Word Pictures in the New Testament, Volume 5* (Broadman Press, 1932), page 408.

77 Barry Joslin, *Hebrews, Christ, and the Law: The Theology of the Mosaic Law in Hebrews* (Paternoster, 2008), page 229.

- Of one's inner inclination to obey God (laws in minds and hearts)
- Of one's firm relationship with God (I will be their God; they will be My people.)
- Of one's knowledge of God (They will know Me.)
- Of one's being forgiven of their sins (I will remember their sins no more.)

The Preacher comes to his point. We are *free from oppression as there is no more guilt*. There is forgiveness, thus no more sacrifice, no more shedding of blood. In the name of Jesus Christ, *you are forgiven*!

And so the Preacher comes to the end of his case for the superiority of Jesus Christ. Throughout his argument he used everything in the Jews' religious life to show the meaning of Jesus's life, death, and resurrection. His challenge was to move his audience toward spiritual maturity and toward God's throne of grace, which was a major life-changing shift from the view of God's throne of judgment! Now, with all that he has stated, what does all this look like in the lives of his audience? The evidence that has been presented requires his audience to make a stand in divine grace, now!

This section consists of four paragraphs, each of which possesses its own distinctive characteristics[78]:

- Verses 19–25,

---

78   William Lane, *World Biblical Commentary, Hebrews 9-13* (Thomas Nelson Publishing, 2000), page 281.

- Verses 26–31,
- Verses 32–35, and
- Verses 36–39

Paragraph 1: Encourage (lest we drift away, chapter 2:1)

The Greek word *parresian*, which the Preacher uses four times in Hebrews, is worth noting. It is translated "boldly" or "confidently," and we can get a sense of the definition as well as the Preacher's point if we look at a passage of scripture in Esther 4:15 through 5:2. One does not go into a king's presence boldly. We notice in the verses that Esther and all the Jews prayed and fasted for Esther that she would be spared and have a meeting with the king, "and if I perish, I perish" (verse 16). Boldly going into the presence of a king was dangerous. But here in Hebrews, the Preacher "depicts the opportunity to address a superior apart from personal fear and apprehension. The believer thus has such boldness 'to enter into the holiest,' namely the heavenly presence of God."[79] In other words, we have been granted access to God and to share our thoughts without fear. We notice that he addresses his audience in each statement as brothers in the family of God ("let us"), something we haven't seen since chapter 3.

"Therefore, brethren, since we have...let us draw near..." The Preacher begins his closing statement of the case for Jesus's

---

79   Robert Gromacki, *Stand Bold in Grace* (Kress Christian Publications, 2002), page 168.

superiority with statements around three major points in this first paragraph:

1. Verse 22: draw near with a sincere heart in *full assurance* of faith
   a. "full assurance"—Greek term *plerophoriai* meaning "most surely believed" (Romans 4:21), "accomplished" (Luke 1:1), and "fully persuaded" (Romans 4:21).

2. Verse 23: hold fast the confession of our hope without *wavering*
   a. "Wavering"—Greek term *akline* means "no leaning," a word picture of a an anchored structure able to withstand the stormiest wind currents.

3. Verse 24: consider how to stimulate one another to love and good deeds
   a. "Consider" is the same word from chapter 3:1— Greek term *katanoomen* referring to one's serious concern and thoughtful perception, contemplating to understand. We encourage one another to love (attitude of the heart), and that our good works are a result, or observable conduct, of our love (Greek *agape* referring to affection or benevolence, Strong's number 26).

Dr. Robert Gromacki states, "The means of provocation are two: association and exhortation (10:25). The pressure of ostracism and the threat of bodily harm had caused some not to attend the congregational meetings of the local church ("as the manner of some is"). The early believers in Jerusalem were together, continuing in fellowship and apostolic instruction (Acts 2:42–44). Weakness comes through division, but togetherness fosters unity and strength. There can be no mutual encouragement if there is separation. Personal interaction of ministry is absolutely necessary. Each member of the body needs the other members (I Corinthians 12:12–26)."[80]

The "day approaching" may lead us to one of two conclusions. First, there are those theologians who view it as the day of Christ's return. Other commentators will point to Jesus's prediction of the fall of Jerusalem and the destruction of the temple by the Romans. The hostilities leading to the Jewish-Roman War (AD 66–73) were very likely present at this time and the discerning Christian could see "the day drawing near."

Paragraph II: Warning (how shall we escape if we neglect so great a salvation, chapter 2:3)

The verses in this paragraph provide the contrast to the verses in paragraph one. As paragraph one was used by the Preacher to show the proper response to Christ's sacrifice, here in this paragraph he presents the improper response to Christ's sacrifice.

In the earliest years of elementary school, I was presented a truth that 2 + 2 equals 4. It is true. One may argue, debate, and research the equation and still come to the truth that 2 +

---

80   Ibid, page 172.

2 equals 4. Four is the sum, and there is no other. If you deny this truth on a test, you will fail the test. There is no other response in which the equation 2 + 2 can be answered. Unless we answer the equation with that which has been presented as the truth, we are without excuse.

In this passage, "there is no lack of understanding of the truth."[81] The Preacher used the same warning we found in chapter 6:4–6. Again using an illustration that his audience would understand, the Preacher reminds them of the result of rejecting (setting aside) the Law of Moses. With testimony from two or three witnesses, the one who rejected the law "dies without mercy" as the punishment.

"The context and parallel with previous passages indicate that the writer has on view the specific sin of apostasy or continuing rejection of Christ."[82] Since the truth of the new covenant is superior, one can only reason that the result of rejecting the truth (salvation in Jesus Christ) is a deserved, more severe punishment. Rejection of the truth reveals one:

1. Trampled *underfoot* the son of God,
2. Has denied that Jesus's blood cleanses us from sin and sanctifies us, and
3. Has insulted the Holy Spirit, our evidence of having received grace.

---

81 Everett Harrison, ed., *The Wycliffe Bible Commentary* (Moody Press, 1962), page 1421.

82 *New Bible Commentary* (InterVarsity Press, 4th edition, 1994), page 1345.

I believe that the term "underfoot" is worth noting. What is the picture of Jesus sitting on His throne according to the Old Testament passage stated in chapter 1:13? Rejection of Jesus, again with no lack of understanding of the truth, shows Jesus as our enemy or as of the One we hold in lowly position (see James 2:1–4). The Preacher ends this paragraph with passages from the LXX (Deuteronomy 32:25–26), and one should be terrified, as it is dreadful to face God when He is acting from the throne of judgment (versus the throne of grace).

Paragraph III: Spiritual achievements (pay much closer attention, chapter 2:1)

I'm reminded of Martin Luther's hymn, *A Mighty Fortress Is Our God*. In the fourth verse is sung:

That word above all earthly powers, no thanks to them, abideth;
The Spirit and the gifts are ours through Him who with us sideth.
Let goods and kindred go, this mortal life also;
The body they may kill: God's truth abideth still,
His Kingdom is forever!"[83]

Remembering past achievements or encounters with God is common in the history of the Jewish faith. In this paragraph the Preacher prompts his audience to remember the beginnings of their own lives after their acceptance of the Gospel. How did his audience respond to crisis and sufferings for their

---

83 From "A Mighty Fortress Is Our God" by Martin Luther (1483-1546).

new faith? They were made "a public spectacle"; the Greek word is *theatrizomenoi*, which is where we get our term "theater." It is a word picture of being put on display or on a stage for all to look upon. We are not given specific details but can understand that for the reason of the display (traitors of the faith by the Jews or anti-emperor worship by the Romans) would indicate that the public spectacle was an attempt to humiliate those on display.

"But remember," says the Preacher, "your response to this persecution." The new believers were sympathetic to fellow believers who had become prisoners for the new faith. The word "sympathetic" (Greek *sumpatheo*) is the same word used to describe our Great High Priest in chapter 4:15. The new believers accepted (Greek *prosdechomai* meaning to receive favorably as by Jesus in Luke 15:2) the seizure (Greek *harpagay* meaning pillage, plundering, extortion, ravening, carry off by force) of their property. With the terms used by the Preacher, we get a picture of believers who were no longer concerned with treasures or their belongings on earth, but were confident in that which God through Jesus Christ had in store for them. They have a "better (Greek *kreitton* meaning nobler) possession (Greek *hooparxis* meaning existence) and an abiding (Greek *meno*, used metaphorically throughout the New Testament to denote an *existing relation* with God, the Holy Spirit, Word of God, other believers, Christ, Christ's love, et al) one."[84] Since you have a nobler existence and a relationship with God, do not throw away,

---

84   James Strong, *The New Strong's Expanded Dictionary of Bible Words* (Thomas Nelson Publishers, 2001), page 1229.

as if it is of no value, your *parresian*, which has a "just recompense" (chapter 2:2).

Paragraph IV: Stay faithful to the saving of the soul!

The Preacher quotes Habakkuk, chapter 2:3–4. Habakkuk was upset over the sin that he thought was so evident. It seemed to him that God was taking no notice of it. But God answers him. God will not delay, but you, being righteous, continue to live by faith. If he (the faithful person) shrinks back—that is, loses faith and becomes fearful—then God has no pleasure (Greek *eudokeo* meaning to approve) in him.

Hebrew Christians, God will not delay. Jesus Christ will return. You believers, keep living by faith even though you are persecuted. We are not like those whose faith shrank; the Preacher is possibly still alluding to those at Kadesh Barnea who did not believe God's promises to them to take the land. We are as those who have faith, believing in Jesus Who preserves (i.e., saves) our soul!

CHAPTER 11
Faithful Lives

We're pilgrims on the journey of the narrow road
And those who've gone before us line the way.
Cheering on the faithful, encouraging the weary;
Their lives a stirring testament to God's sustaining grace.

Surrounded by so great a cloud of witnesses,
Let us run the race not only for the prize.
But as those who've gone before us, let us leave to those be-
hind us
A heritage of faithfulness passed down through godly lives.

Oh may all who come behind us find us faithful!
May the fire of our devotion light their way.
May the footprints that we leave
Lead them to believe.
And the lives we live inspire them to obey.
Oh may all who come behind us find us faithful![85]

---

85   Jon Mohr, "Find Us Faithful." © 1987 Birdwing Music.

If he was available at the time, I'm sure Steve Green would have been asked to sing Jon Mohr's song, "Find Us Faithful," to the Preacher's audience. The Preacher has concluded his statement that we are "those who have faith to the preserving of the soul." In his manner of using Israel's past to enlighten his present message, he now points to Israel's "men of old" (verse 2, NASB) to bring his audience to an understanding of living by faith. His audience needs to see, or be reminded of, the life of faith they are encouraged to live. Israel has a history of persons who lived faithfully even though they were persecuted, or obeyed faithfully even though they had no real understanding as to the fullness of what they were being asked to do. The Preacher makes his case for what faith reveals. The Preacher's audience needed encouragement to endure patiently through their trials and persecution. In the first verse of chapter 11, he is giving a principle of faith. There is neither a specific descriptive term used with the word "faith," such as Christian faith, nor is there a definite article "the." His statement is not defining faith but rather what faith reveals: "substance" and "conviction."

We first note the Greek terms used for "substance" (*huposta-sis*) and "conviction" (*elegchos*). The Greek term *elegchos* can also be translated as "proof." We have seen the word *hupos-tasis* in chapter 1:3 translated as "nature" in that verse. The word *hupostasis* is defined as "what stands under anything (a building, a contract, a promise). We venture to suggest the translation "Faith is the *title deed* of things hoped for."[86] Along

---

86   A. T. Robertson, *Word Pictures of the New Testament, Volume 5* (Broadman Press, 1932), page 418.

with this, the verse associates "hoped for" with substance. In Biblical texts, the word "hope" is never a wish, a dream, or a fantasy. Hope is that *settled assurance* (italics are mine) that comes to the child of God who by faith lays hold of promises of God and claims them for himself.[87]

Our faith then reveals our assurance that God's promises are true and lasting. Our faith also reveals proof of our trust in what is unseen. We note that our conviction is *trust in the unseen, not the unknown.*[88] We see nature and know it was created by God. Like Job, we have never commanded the morning and caused the dawn to know its place. We do not understand the expanse of the earth. We have never entered the storehouses of snow or hail. We have not put wisdom in the innermost being or have given understanding to the mind. It is not by our command that the eagle mounts up and makes his nest on high (Job chapters 38 and 39). We know that God created that which is seen by the mere "word" (Greek *rhema* meaning "utterance") of His command.

Our faith, Hebrews, knows that God's promises are true. The Holy Spirit in us is proof of our intimate relationship with God through Jesus Christ. We trust *in the reality* of what is unseen! Because our sins are not merely covered but are forgiven, we know God and He knows us! Because of our faith in God's promises, because we have faith in that which is unseen, *our faith then naturally enables us to patiently endure.*

---

87 J. Dwight Pentecost, *Faith That Endures* (Kregel Publications, 1992), page 175.
88 Everett Harrison, ed., *The Wycliffe Bible Commentary* (Moody Press, 1962), page 1421.

Without faith, it is impossible to please God. The Preacher cites a number of historical figures as examples of faith and how it pleases God. The first person mentioned is Abel. We know that scripture says he gave of the fat portions of the firstlings of his flock compared to Cain's offering, which was from his work with the ground (an offering of "the fruit of the ground," Genesis 4:3–4). God was pleased with Abel's offering but not with Cain's. Some commentaries will show statements that Abel knew the Lord wanted sacrifices, but we see no evidence of this. The only hint as to why God was pleased with Abel and not Cain comes in Genesis 4:7 when the Lord tells Cain that if he does "well" (Hebrews *yatab*), Cain's countenance will be lifted up. The Hebrew word *yatab* does not mean to amend nor improve your ways, but to make one's course line up with that which is pleasing to God and that which is well pleasing in His sight.[89] With this in mind, we can see Abel's mind-set was to please God, and God was certainly pleased with Abel. Also, Abel's sacrifice was "a more sacrifice" (Greek *pleiona thusian*), which is the same terminology used in Matthew 5:20 to say that one's righteousness must exceed that of the scribes and Pharisees, as well as in Luke 21:3 when it is used to describe the widow's mites compared to the amount given by the rich. The mind-set of the faithful shows "one's course lines up with that which is pleasing to God!"

Moses mentions Enoch in the descendants of Adam through his son Seth. In Genesis chapter 5, we learn that Adam was

---

89 James Strong, *The New Strong's Expanded Dictionary of Bible Words* (Thomas Nelson Publishers, 2001), page 516.

Seth's father. Seth was the father of Enosh. Enosh's son was Kenan. Kenan became the father of Mahalalel. Mahalalel's son was Jared, and Jared was Enoch's father. Enoch "walked with God" for 365 years, and then God "took him." Enoch did not die. We get an idea that Enoch's walk with God was one that lined up with that which is pleasing to God, as in the original Hebrew a definite article comes before "God" in verses 22 and 24. We're not told the specifics of Enoch's life, but in view of the original Hebrew, a definitive article before "God" would indicate (e.g., Daniel 4:2 where Nebuchadnezzar refers to God as the "Most High God") people worshipping other gods or idols. Enoch's course was to walk with the true and living God.

The last preflood person of faith the Preacher cites is Noah. To my thinking, Noah is a perfect example of believing in the reality of things unseen and patient endurance. Imagine being told to build an ark because there will come a flood to destroy the earth. We don't have record that Noah asked God to define "flood," nor do we know if Noah asked God to define "rain." Noah built the ark "in reverence" (Greek *eulabeomai*), meaning that Noah built the ark in holy fear of that which was going to happen. Having no idea of how the flood would occur (it had never rained), he defied and condemned the world with his building and believed in the reality of that which did occur 125 years later. In Genesis 6:22, Moses states, "Thus Noah did; according to all that God had commanded him, so he did." (NASB)

We see in these preflood figures that their life's course was set to that (faith) which is pleasing to God. As the Preacher mentions in verse 6, "Without faith it is impossible to please Him, for he who comes to God must believe that He is, and that He is a rewarder of those who seek Him." (NASB)

From the preflood era, the Preacher now highlights the Patriarchs. We will note the Preacher's remark that the Patriarchs "confessed" (NASB, Greek *homologeo*) that they were "strangers and exiles" while on the earth (verse 13), which "is all of a piece with the underlying principle of the Epistle that it is the heavenly and not the earthly things which are most important."[90] The Greek term *homologeo* is a picture of one agreeing to and confessing a deep conviction of the facts.[91] Their status as "strangers and exiles on the earth" was demonstrated by the fact they lived in tents (see verse 9). Abraham was "looking for" (Greek *ekdechomai* meaning to await, expect, suggests reaching out in readiness to receive something[92]) the city that has foundations whose "craftsman" and "builder" (Greek *demiourgos*, emphasizing the power of a Divine creator[93]) is God (Greek *theos* meaning supreme divinity, denotes the *one true God*[94]).

The faith of the Patriarchs begins, naturally, with father Abraham. In the chapter 11 passages, the Preacher describes the evidence of Abraham's faith. First, he obeyed (verse 8, Greek *hupakouo*). The word for "obeyed" is a picture of one not just

---

90 Donald Guthrie, *Hebrews* (InterVarsity Press, 1983), page 236.
91 James Strong, *The New Strong's Expanded Dictionary of Bible Words* (Thomas Nelson Publishers, 2001), page 1268.
92 Ibid, page 1066.
93 Ibid, page 1035.
94 Ibid, page 1137.

doing as he is told, but *actively listening so he responds and conforms to the command*. He was instructed to leave Ur, his home, and go to the land that God had promised to him and his descendants (Genesis 15:5). We notice that Abram believed God when told he would have descendants, even before God made His covenant with him (Genesis 15:6–21). Now this belief that he would have descendants came from an unshakable faith: Abraham and his wife, Sarah, were well past childbearing age, and at this point in their lives, they had had no children. The Preacher mentions that Abraham was "as good as dead at that" (NASB, Greek *nekroo* passively meaning "deprived of power"[95]), referring to his ability to procreate (verse 12).

So Abraham and Sarah considered God faithful. Isaac was born to them, and it was "in Isaac your (Abraham) descendants shall be called" (Genesis 21:12). Having one offspring with Sarah, and through that offspring his descendants would come, Abraham by faith and as instructed by God offered up Isaac as a sacrifice (Genesis 22). We notice that faith broadens one's trust in God: Abraham not only believes that his descendants would come through Isaac whom God gave to him and his wife, but additionally now God is able to raise men even from the dead (Greek *nekros* meaning death of the body[96]). "Because of Abraham's faith, the prospect of losing Isaac did not force him to give up or lose his grip on God's promise; it actually refined his faith, teaching him about the possibility of resurrection."[97]

---

95   James Strong, *The New Strong's Expanded Dictionary of Bible Words* (Thomas Nelson Publishers, 2001), page 1250.

96   Ibid.

97   Thomas G. Long, *Hebrews: Interpretation* (Westminster John Knox Press, 1997),

The Preacher mentions that Isaac (Genesis 26:2–4) and Jacob (Genesis 35:9–12) were heirs of the same promise made to Abraham. A key word in passages 20 and 21 is the word "blessed," which comes from the Greek *eulogeo*, giving a picture of one passing on one's prosperity from God. If Isaac and Jacob did not believe God's promise, there would have been no continued blessing. Joseph, if he did not believe, would have had no reason to ask to rebury his bones in the Promised Land.

These all "died in faith without receiving the promises...but welcomed them from a distance..." Beginning with verse 13, J. B. Phillips's English translation reads:

> All these whom we have mentioned maintained their faith but died without actually receiving God's promises, though they had seen them in the distance, had hailed them as true. They freely admitted that they lived on this earth as exiles and foreigners. Men who say that mean, of course, that their eyes are fixed upon their true homeland. If they had meant the particular country they had left behind (*as their homeland*), they had ample opportunity to return. No, the fact is that they longed for a better country altogether, nothing less than a *heavenly one*. And because of this faith of theirs, God is not ashamed to be called their God (see chapter 2:11) for He has prepared for them a city.[98] (Italics are mine.)

---

page 120.

98   J. B. Phillips, *The New Testament in Modern English* (Galahad Books, 1958), pages 471–472.

The patriarchs exemplified the spiritual vision, or relationship, of faith. We see that the faith of the patriarchs never wavered from the "assurance of things hoped for." They remained true to God, believing that He would do what He said He would do. It wasn't man in whom they placed their hope; it was the one true God.

The Preacher continues with the faith exemplified by Moses starting in verse 23. The people of Israel are now in Egypt (Genesis 15:13). We understand faith was first demonstrated by Moses's parents (both from the house of Levi, see Exodus chapter 2). Pharaoh commanded, "Every son who is born you are to cast into the Nile, and every daughter you are to keep alive" (see Exodus chapter 1). The parents showed their faith in God by showing no fear of the king's edict that a newborn son was to be put to death. Eventually their son was "cast into the Nile" only in a manner that Pharaoh did not have in mind!

Where the faith of the patriarchs reveals trust in the unseen and how faith is refined, the faith of Moses adds a perspective that faith endures "ill treatment" (verse 25). Moses had a choice; he could have been living comfortably with great earthly treasures and position, but instead he chose "rather to endure ill-treatment with the people of God than to enjoy the passing pleasures of sin."

The Preacher is leading his audience to "follow the leader." The patriarchs showed their trust in the reality of the unseen. "Now, Hebrews," says the Preacher, "look at Moses. He considered 'the reproach of Christ' (i.e., being ill-treated because of belief in the Messiah) over the wealth offered him through an Egyptian life, because he placed his trust in the assurance that God's promises are true and lasting." We learn that Moses's faith did not deny that there was a Pharaoh and his edicts or deny that there was wrath placed on the Israelite slaves, those of whom Moses chose over the Egyptian life. "Simply, Hebrews, *faith sees God* not the oppressors, and takes God at His word," the Preacher reveals to his audience.

It was by faith that the Red Sea parted, allowing passage for the Israelites on dry land, yet drowning the Egyptian army. It was by faith that the walls of Jericho fell. By faith, acknowledging "the Lord your God is God in heaven above and on earth beneath" (Joshua 2:11), Rahab and her family were spared.

There are more stories of faithful ancestors to share; however, the Preacher merely highlights their acts, which include:

- Conquering kingdoms (e.g., Judges 4, Barak and Deborah)
- Showing acts of righteousness (e.g., II Samuel 8:15, David; I Samuel 12:4, Samuel)
- Obtaining promises (e.g., II Samuel 7:8–17)
- Shutting the mouths of lions (e.g., Judges 14:6, Samson)
- Quenching the power of fire (e.g., Daniel 3:23, Shadrach, Meshach, and Abed-nego)
- Women receiving blessings in response to their faithfulness (e.g. I Kings 17:17-24, Elijah and the widow's son)

Once we think we've had enough examples of faith, the Preacher's list continues merely stating "others" and persecution even to death that was experienced by these persons of whom "the world was not worthy." These all "gained approval" (Greek *martureo* meaning "to bear witness to" and sometimes rendered "to testify"[99]); their faith bore witness to our one true God.

Ending this section of faith shown in the men of old, the Preacher notes that these others, as the patriarchs, died in faith without receiving the promises. His last statement (verse 40) is a real challenge to his audience and to us today. Apart from us, they will not be "made perfect" (Greek *teleioo* meaning "to complete, consummate"[100]). The faith of the men of old has been passed down through generations. Their faith revealed their hope in God's promises. Their faith was one that sees God and sees beyond oppression even to the point of death. We complete their faith by being faithful to God ourselves.

He has provided "something better" for us: remember "better than the angels," "better hope," "better covenant," "better promises," and "better sacrifice." In this lies the truth regarding "apart from us." We look at this statement spiritually; the men of old were worshipping in temporary structures and repeating sacrifices. They were looking ahead to something better! By Jesus we are all tied together through the ages, a line

---

99   James Strong, *The New Strong's Expanded Dictionary of Bible Words* (Thomas Nelson Publishers, 2001), page 1222.
100 Ibid, page 1409.

of the faithful from the beginning of human history to today. This connecting line is the "hope set before us. This hope we have is an anchor of the soul, a hope both sure and steadfast and one which enters within the veil, where Jesus has entered as a forerunner for us, having become a high priest forever according to the order of Melchizedek" (chapter 6:18–20).

If we listen closely, we may hear the Preacher leading his audience:

Oh may all who come behind us find us faithful!
May the fire of our devotion light their way.
May the footprints that we leave lead them to believe
And the lives we live inspire them to obey.
Oh may all who come behind us find us faithful!

CHAPTER 12
Support Each Other

Let's review some of what the Preacher has presented. We learned at the beginning of our study in chapter 1 that "God spoke to us through Son!"

> God spoke through prophets or angels, but Jesus, the incarnate identity of God, is even greater! To which of the angels did God ever call His Son? Only Jesus Christ is God. Jesus then, being God, is a more excellent way. Focus your attention, Hebrews, on who Jesus is! "We shall not escape" such a great salvation, which is so great "because it makes saints out of sinners!"[101]

From chapter 2 of our study, we tried to put ourselves in the audience's shoes as we learned:

> Many if not most of the audience came from Jewish

---

101 Robert Gromacki, *Stand Bold in Grace* (Kress Christian Publications, 2002), page 41.

education. Believing in Jesus as the Messiah at that time was much different than it is today. I don't believe we understand what they understood about the Crucifixion in their time and culture. "We easily forget that the central narrative of the Christian faith is, on the face of it, a deep embarrassment. Often we have turned the passion story into harmless sentiment and the cross into a piece of jewelry, losing touch with what early Christians painfully knew, that Jesus died in shame and that the cross is, to reasonable eyes, an inexplicable foolishness and a stumbling block to faith. No wonder the Preacher had taken such pains earlier to contrast the Son to angels, to emphasize that, when the full truth is known, Jesus the Son is higher than the angels."[102] There always was with the audience a danger that under the stressful conditions of persecution they would give up on their faith. So the Preacher's message is hold on to your faith! Remember, a true confession of Christ is priority one! We can see the shame of the Crucifixion; however, focus on the *life that His death brings*! God intends to give us salvation as a permanent possession, we must be all the more attentive to what He and others have said about it.[103]

Chapter 6 begins with the Preacher leading his audience to move forward "to the goal set for us by God" (verse 1):

That is the meaning of the word "maturity" (*teliotes*,

---

102 Thomas G. Long, *Hebrews: Interpretation* (Westminster John Knox Press, 1997), pages 25–26.
103 Paul Ellingsworth, *Commentary on Hebrews, New International Greek Testament Commentary* (Eerdmans, 1993), page 135.

meaning "goal"or "purpose"). The Preacher doesn't want to repeat the foundations of salvation. "Going back to the foundations will not help those who have *deliberately turned away* from God."[104] Let's move forward to maturity.

There have been those who did not move forward toward maturity, who turned away from God. They knew the foundations of salvation. These persons were enlightened in that they received and accepted the saving grace of God through Jesus's death and resurrection. They understood salvation by grace and not works, or in keeping the law. The terms the Preacher uses show that these people were knowledgeable and participated even in miracles. It is not specifically clear that the Preacher was speaking of individuals in his audience, but some believers (at least in general) had "fallen away" (*parapipto*); that is "apostatized," a *willing reversal* to the adherence to the realities and facts of the faith.[105] The Preacher is trying to make his point; it was the Preacher's "purpose to portray extreme peril so that those tempted to apostasy might have the strongest possible example."[106] I'm reminded of the words the Apostle Paul used as he "encouraged" his readers in his letter to the church in Galatia: "you stupid Galatians," "oh, you dear idiots of Galatia," "you foolish Galatians," etc. (Galatians 3:1, from different versions/

104 J. B. Phillips, *The New Testament in Modern English* (Glahad Books , 1958), page 461.
105 James Strong, *The New Strong's Expanded Dictionary of Bible Words* (Nelson Publishers, 2001), page 1293.
106 Everett Harrison, ed., *The Wycliffe Bible Commentary* (Moody Press, 1962), page 1415.

translations). One does not use gentle terms when dealing with apostasy!

Now as we begin chapter 12, the Preacher has made his point that through Jesus we are all tied together through the ages, a line of the faithful from the beginning of human history. We can imagine the Preacher saying, "Young Christians, remain faithful and complete the faith of your fathers, for they too were challenged and persecuted! You are not experiencing anything new that comes with being faithful. Jesus is God incarnate. Remember the life that His death on the cross brings, remember why it was fitting for Him to suffer, and remember He endured hostility against Himself! Don't lose heart! Don't turn away!"

Just as the Preacher has been pointing his audience to think of our relationship with God *spiritually*, he now introduces how we can spiritually understand enduring our circumstances. Discipline is the key word in verses 4 through 13 after sharing about the "great cloud of witnesses." The term used in verse 1 for "witness" is the Greek word *martus*, from where we get our word "martyr" as one who bears witness by his death. "Hebrews 12:1, '(a cloud) of witnesses' here is of those mentioned in chapter 11, those whose lives and actions testified to the worth and effect of faith."[107] Keeping in mind the evidence showing their endurance, the Preacher gives his audience three appeals. He uses athletic competition to help his audience identify with discipline:

---

107 W. E. Vine, *Vine's Complete Expository Dictionary* (Thomas Nelson Publishers, 1984), pages 680–681.

1. Lay aside every encumbrance,
2. Lay aside "the sin" (note the article prior to the word "sin"), and
3. Run the race with endurance.

The Preacher uses the term "lay aside" in two appeals. The first is to lay aside "every encumbrance," and the second is to lay aside "the sin." The term "lay aside" is the same wording that Paul uses in Romans 13:12 and is a picture of taking off a robe. When Stephen was stoned (Acts 7), Saul was said to be holding robes that were "laid aside" as the robes encumbered one's efforts to throw stones. We see an athlete in training to run a race and win. We remember from chapter 2:

> To this end, the Preacher begins with nautical terms, telling the audience that "we must pay more attention so that we do not drift away." These terms "arrest the attention of the reader with a strong warning."[108] With the use of the Greek terms *dei* (must, literally "it is necessary") with the adverb *perissoteros* (more careful), followed by *prosecho* (pay attention) and *pararuomen* (drift away) the Preacher gives a word picture that it's not just logical but both logical and morally necessary. A pilot of a ship is steering the ship to port. There were no motors on ships! You miss the port and it may be days before you get another chance to dock your ship. It is a picture of a ship's pilot who is not only mindful of the swift currents, but he is convinced that there is no plan B. He *will* guide the ship to port on

---

108 David L. Allen, *NIV The New American Commentary, Hebrews* (B & H Publishing Group, 2010), page 191.

the first attempt despite the currents. The ship will be then be "fastened to the seabed" (*prosechein*) to be kept from drifting.

When I think of striving to avoid carelessness, I'm reminded of Paul's message to run a race (I Corinthians 9:24–27). His analogy was of one training for games. The Greek term for "games" is *agonizomai*, the word from which we get our English words "agony" and "agonize." It sets in mind a specific task that involves training with the mindset to achieve nothing less than first place. We earnestly heed the things that we have heard with the intention to achieve nothing less than being steadfast in our faith. We are earnest so that we will not give up or drift away. There is neither placing second in the race nor missing the dock!

So the athlete agonizes to train and condition his or her body to achieve winning the race (e.g., in training the athlete sheds excess weight). The athlete concentrates and focuses on the goal and not on the taunts by the competitors. One of the encumbrances the Preacher's audience will have to lay aside is the taunting persecution from its enemies.

In the second appeal, the Preacher says to "lay aside the sin," and we notice the article "the" showing that the Preacher is referring to a specific sin. It is not any sin, but he is referring to the particular sin of "falling away," of which he has been appealing to his audience (chapter 6). Lay aside the desire to return to the law or temple activities.

The third appeal is to "run with endurance" (Greek *hupomone* meaning "patient continuance") the "race" (Greek *agon*, implying one's agonizing in a contest, conflict, contention, fight, or race) that is set before us. What is that race? The race we are enduring is *our effort to become mature Christians*, to stay away from apostasy (result of *the* sin). The race is to achieve Christian maturity!

"People can endure intense distress and pain if they know it is not meaningless."[109] "Fix our eyes" and "consider Jesus," the Preacher implores in verses 2 and 3 as he did in chapter 3 ("fix our eyes," Greek *aphorao* meaning to be attentive; and "consider," Greek *homologeo* would be like grabbing a person from the lapels and saying, "Listen up and pay attention!"). "Yes, think about Him who endured such hostility against Himself from sinners, so that you won't grow tired and become despondent (literally 'fainting in your souls')."[110]

"What does persecution have to do with one's maturity?" his audience may ask. We notice in verse 4 that the Preacher is telling those in his audience that they have "yet" to be martyrs and have forgotten "the exhortation which is addressed to you as sons" (NASB). Note the interesting use of the word "yet," as if the Preacher is implying that the time for their martyrdom is coming. The forgotten exhortation comes from Proverbs 3:11–12. The key phrase in the passage is "discipline of the

---

109 Thomas G. Long, *Hebrews: Interpretation* (Westminster John Knox Press, 1997), page 132.
110 David H. Stern, *Complete Jewish Bible* (Jewish New Testament Publications, Inc., 1988), Messianic Jews (Hebrews) 12:3, page 1507.

Lord." The persecution that is being experienced is the Lord's disciplining of his sons.

The Greek word for "discipline" that the Preacher uses is *paideuo* meaning to *train* up a child, i.e., *educate, teach, instruct, chastise.*[111] In verse 6 the Preacher quotes that God "scourges" every son. The Greek term for "scourges" is *mastigoo* and is used metaphorically in Hebrews 12:6 to tell of the chastening by the Lord, administered in love to His spiritual sons.[112] This text does not refer to the method, as described in II Corinthians 11:24 administered to Paul, of using the three thongs of leather (forty stripes save one) to inflict thirteen stripes on the bare breast and thirteen on each shoulder.[113]

Why do good parents (including God) discipline their children? The answer is that good parents exercise discipline because they want their children to grow up to be like them, to share their values, commitments, and way of life.[114] What can we realize from persecution? Jesus Himself was scorned and persecuted, and it is said that "it was fitting for Him for whom are all things, and through whom are all things, in bringing many sons to glory, to perfect the Author of their salvation through sufferings" (chapter 3:10). We learned that Noah was ridiculed and taunted while building the ark for 125 years. Abraham and his sons lived in tents in the land God was promising to them and their descendants. Joseph

---

111 James Strong, *The New Strong's Expanded Dictionary of Bible Words* (Nelson Publishers, 2001), page 1282.
112 Ibid, page 1223.
113 Ibid.
114 Thomas G. Long, *Hebrews: Interpretation* (Westminster John Knox Press, 1997), page 133.

suffered years in Egypt after being taunted by his own brothers before he matured to the point that God was able to use him for His glory. Moses left Egypt fearing the wrath of the king. Samson lived through the taunts and persecution of the Philistines. David was persecuted by King Saul for twelve years before he became king. Hebrews, martyrdom is yet to come!

We realize that through God's loving discipline (persecution, trials), our faith is made perfect because it leads us to focus on the life that Jesus's death brings. It leads us to maturity in Christ. It is for our good so that we may share His holiness (verse 10). We can appreciate the Preacher's words in verse 11 that at the moment it is not joyful but sorrowful when learning from being disciplined, yet it "yields the 'peaceful' (Greek *eirenikos* meaning peaceful communication with God[115]) fruit of 'righteousness'"(Greek *dikaiosune* meaning to have the character or quality of being right or just with God[116]). Realize then, Hebrews, that God disciplines those He loves.

Discipline (teaching through persecution) is necessary lest we become unfocused and at best to help us learn a "path of least resistance" that leads to spiritual death. We remember from chapter 2 that there was always within the audience the fear that under the stressful conditions of persecution they would give up on their faith. So the Preacher's message continues to be to hold on to your faith and accept the Lord's discipline.

---

115 James Strong, *The New Strong's Expanded Dictionary of Bible Words* (Nelson Publishers, 2001), page 1062.
116 Ibid, page 1044.

A true confession of Christ is priority one! Remember from chapter 6, to fall away is to reject Jesus and reaffirm the view of Jesus's enemies that He deserved to die on a cross.

Beginning with verse 12, we recognize the words "therefore" and "but" as words that prompt us to think that what is about to be presented is dependent on what has just been presented. We will see these words three times from verse 12 through the end of this chapter. In verse 12, "therefore" now shifts our minds from understanding the Preacher's definition of "discipline" to understanding our roles as God's children as we grow toward spiritual maturity. We want to pay attention to key words in verses 12 through 17 of this chapter that are worth examining.

From the NASB, we have:

- Verse 12—*strengthen, lame*
- Verse 13—*make straight*
- Verse 14—*peace*
- Verse 14—*sanctification*
- Verse 15—*see to it*
- Verse 15—*springing up*
- Verse 16—*immoral, godless person*

"Strengthen" is the Greek word *anorthoo*, which is a word picture of making upright someone whose posture is slumped over. "Lame" is the Greek word *paralelumena* meaning "paralyzed." Together these words paint a picture of someone who is so depressed or fearful that his or her whole countenance, physically and mentally, shows that he or she has no energy or ability to move. As if in a race (remember the analogy beginning in 12:1), the person can't go on. We want to make straight paths; the Greek word for "straight" is *orthos*, coming from the root word *oros*. *Orthos* refers to "honest," "level," or "direct," along with *oros*, which refers proverbially to overcoming difficulties, or accomplishing great things.[117] They present a picture, such as what Paul used in Galatians 2:14, where one travels a course of conduct that leaves a path for others to follow. We see the Preacher saying, "Just as those who've traveled a faithful path before us ("great cloud of witness") are an inspiration to us, let us (audience) be a present inspiration to each other!"

How can we inspire and encourage? We pursue "peace" (*eirene*) and "sanctification." Sanctification describes one being "set apart by God to God's benefit." The word "sanctification" is the Greek word *hagiasmos*, which signifies "purity" and "holiness." In this passage from the Preacher, it is not merely a state of being but a continuing act of desiring and purposefully progressing toward the conduct God calls, through his grace, for believers to live. The Preacher is stressing for each of us to show such purpose in the paths we travel. We "see to it" (the Greek word *episkopeo*, which refers to a *willful,* careful, and diligent awareness. We willfully watch each other, and because of the peace we have with each other, we willfully depend on others to watch us so that we stay upright as we walk on the straight path revealing God's grace.

---

117 James Strong, *The New Strong's Expanded Dictionary of Bible Words* (Nelson Publishers, 2001), page 1274.

There are three objectives the Preacher mentions for which we are to watch. The first is that "no one comes short of the grace of God (NASB)." To "come up short" is the Greek word *hustereo*, which is a picture of someone who is deficient of something. The second is that "no root of bitterness springing up causes trouble and by it many be defiled." "Springing up" is the Greek word *phuo*, along with *ano*; it refers to something unintentional growing up that becomes overshadowing to the point that it is now the point of focus. In the third, the Preacher points us to Esau. Esau is described as "immoral" (Greek *pornos*) and a "godless person" (Greek *bebelos*). *Pornos* refers to seeking one's fleshly satisfaction and *bebelos* refers to one who is profane, the antonym of sanctification. The example of Esau is not so much saying that he was sexually immoral, but that his birthright (God's blessing) had no meaning to him; even his fleshly desire to satisfy his hunger for one meal meant more!

The Preacher's audience is seeking familiar ground. Because of intense persecution, they are seeking a refuge by returning to practicing the faith of their lives before their confession of faith in Jesus. Just as the Preacher used strong terms previously to warn against apostasy, he now compares, with the strongest illustration, Mount Sinai and Mount Zion. We notice that Mount Sinai is not mentioned by name but only through the use of Old Testament passages. It's like his audience is at a fork in the road: you can return to Mount Sinai or stay the course to Mount Zion.

"Audience, we remember that we now approach God's throne

of grace (Zion) and not God's throne of judgment (Sinai). Do you really want to go back to the past and meet God with fear? Do you really want to deny your perfection (salvation) in Jesus? Remember when God physically met the Israelites on Mount Sinai? Even Moses (Deuteronomy 9:19) was full of fear at the sound of God's voice. So intimidating was the presence and voice of God that those there begged that God would only speak to them through Moses. While in God's presence on the mountain, the command that even if an animal (wild or one appointed for sacrifice) touches the mountain it will be stoned (to death) was more than they could endure," the Preacher explains. Beginning in verse 22, the Preacher begins with the word "but" just as in verse 12 he used the word "therefore." What is to follow about Mount Zion comes with the understanding of what has been said about Mount Sinai. The Preacher continues, "Look to where we have come, to the heavenly (not physical) true city of the living God! We have come to God's throne of grace!"

J. B. Phillips writes, "You have drawn near to the countless angelic army, the assembly of the Church of the firstborn whose names are written in Heaven. You have drawn near to Jesus..."[118]

It is Jesus the mediator (Greek *mesites* referring to one who mediates between two parties with a view to produce a peaceful relation[119]) of the new covenant (versus the old covenant

---

118 J. B. Phillips, *The New Testament in Modern English* (Galahad Books, 1958), page 475.
119 Ibid, page 1230.

as at Mount Sinai) whose cleansing blood delivers its message (of salvation) better than the blood of Abel (delivered its message of judgment)! Jesus's blood is speaking, "Do not refuse Him who is speaking" (NASB, verse 25).

If there was no escaping the warnings from earth (e.g., see Genesis 18:20 through 19:29), then those who fall away will not escape the warnings from heaven! "How shall we escape if we neglect such a great salvation (chapter 2:3)?" The phrase in verse 25 is stated unlike the passage in chapter 2. In chapter 2, it is rhetorical, having the force of a strong negative meaning "we shall not escape!" This time the Preacher leaves no doubt; for apostasy, there is no escape from judgment. The Preacher quotes Haggai 2:6 in which God says, "Once more in a little while, I am going to shake the heavens and the earth." We also want to see that just prior to verse 6 in Haggai 2, God says, "My Spirit is abiding in your midst; do not fear!" Separating good from evil is not uncommon in scripture. Jesus tells how the wind separated the wheat from the chaff (e.g., Psalm 1:4) or how fire will destroy the chaff (Matthew 3:12). Fire refines gold by bringing the dross to the top to be skimmed off so all that is left is pure gold (e.g., Malachi 3:3). God will separate that which can be shaken (ungodly) from that which cannot be shaken (sanctified).

Since we are a part of that which is unshakable, we show gratitude (Greek *charis*, a word picture of one's manner or acts of thanks, figuratively or spiritually, in response to the divine influence upon the heart and its reflection in one's life[120]).

120 James Strong, *The New Strong's Expanded Dictionary of Bible Words* (Nelson

We note that this gratitude by definition is a response to God: without His influence *first*, we cannot show *charis*.

Chapter 12 finishes with the Preacher quoting Deuteronomy 4:24: "For the Lord your God is a consuming fire." The word "consuming" is a combination of the Greek words *analisko*, which means to use up or spend up, especially in a bad sense,[121] and *katanarkao*, which means to consume utterly, wholly.[122] We have then a picture of God who purifies all that is unworthy and unacceptable in those who serve Him and all that is unfit to abide in His presence.[123]

At this point, the Preacher finishes his sermon. We will see in the remaining verses (chapter 13) exhortations, mostly disconnected from his main theme, as well as the Preacher's benediction. Before we study his last words, we remind ourselves of his lessons to this point:

> We are now in Jesus Christ. Being in Jesus, God sees us as perfect. Our sins are forgiven, not merely covered until the next Day of Atonement. We strive toward spiritual maturity, as we realize that through God's loving discipline our faith is made perfect; His discipline leads us to focus on the life that Jesus's death brings. We come to God's throne of grace and no longer to His throne of judgment. Our lives reveal conduct to which God calls His believers to live. We willfully watch each other, and because of the

Publishers, 2001), page 1451.

121 Ibid, page 946.
122 Ibid, page 1171.
123 J. Dwight Pentecost, *Faith That Endures* (Kregel Publications, 1992), page 213.

peace we have with each other, we willfully depend on others to watch us so that we stay upright as we walk on the straight path revealing God's grace. We look without fear to the day when God will finally separate the evil from good. In response to His grace and His influence upon our hearts; being cleansed by the blood of Jesus and having been filled with His Spirit, we are able to hold fast to our confession of faith. With gratitude to God, we worship Him in true reverence and awe.

CHAPTER 13
Final Words
from the Preacher

The Preacher, having concluded his main theme, ends his message by encouraging his audience with advice for practical behavior. These items to come in this chapter may be thought of as being disconnected from the formal material in the previous twelve chapters. These are meant to directing Christians in their congregational and daily lives. We see three sections in this last text from the Preacher:

1. Love that supports one another,
2. Faith and conduct pleasing to God, and
3. Benediction

Love that supports
The Preacher begins by exhorting his audience to continue their "love of the brethren" (NASB), to "show hospitality," to

"honor marriage," and to allow character that is "free from the love of money" (13:1–6). I like the way the Preacher mentions the Greek term *philadelphia* for starters. "That's easy enough," I would expect the response to be. Of course it is easy to love those with whom you associate. It's easy to love those who show love to you. But after opening with instruction that even nonbelievers would agree with, the Preacher moves on with character traits of love that are demonstrated in those who are sanctified. Perhaps not as easy as loving those who love you is to show hospitality to strangers and show empathy to prisoners.

The Preacher mentions that in showing hospitality to strangers, one may "unwittingly" (Greek *lanthano*) be entertaining angels, having in mind Abraham's experience in Genesis 18. The third-century church order *Didascalia* gives instructions to bishops about the kind of ready hospitality they should show if a stranger should unexpectedly arrive at the assembly:

> "If a destitute man or woman, either a local person or a traveler, arrives unexpectedly, especially one of older years, and there is no place, you, bishop, make such a place with all your heart, even if you yourself should sit on the ground, that you many not show favoritism among human beings, but that your ministry may be pleasing to God."[124]

As they, the audience, were outcasts, then certainly empathy

---

124 Thomas G. Long, *Hebrews: Interpretation* (Westminster John Knox Press, 1997), page 143.

would be expressed toward those who were imprisoned and ill-treated. The exhortation conveys the act of one identifying with the imprisoned. The picture is that the one ministering is just as likely to be imprisoned as the one to whom he is ministering. The beliefs or actions for which they were imprisoned are the same beliefs and actions that we share!

The Preacher gives critical advice toward the Christian view of marriage. This topic may seem disconnected from his main theme to us; however, we remember that the audience was Hebrew. Depending on what rabbi's teaching you followed, you may approach the matter of marriage with leniency, as in the teaching of Rabbi Hillel who taught that a woman was man's property and could be dismissed for any reason including that the man may find another woman more physically attractive. Those who followed the teaching of another popular rabbi, Shammai (Hillel's contemporary and, at times, adversary), would approach marriage more strictly. Conventional thought at the time included tolerance of fornication and adultery.

Many or most of these people had suffered the loss of possessions. The Preacher warns them to "be free from the love of money" (Greek *aphilargyros* meaning "not money loving" rather than "not covetous"[125]). We remember all that has been taught thus far, the direct presence of God through Jesus Christ our High Priest. We have been made perfect in Jesus Christ. Seek comfort then from God's presence and His provision!

---

125 Everett Harrison, ed., *The Wycliffe Bible Commentary* (Moody Press, 1962), page 1426.

Show that we are set apart, sanctified. God's holiness and purity can be demonstrated by our attitudes and behavior as we seek continued fellowship with our brethren, show hospitality and empathy, show honor in marriage, and contentment in our relationship with God through Jesus Christ. By such we profess with confidence that found in Psalm 118:6: "The Lord is my Helper, I will not be afraid. What shall man do to me?" Such a question is termed as in chapter 2:3 in such as way as to lead to a negative response; man cannot separate me from God!

Pleasing to God

The Christians are encouraged to remember those "who led" them—Greek *hegeomai* meaning to lead with authority; "authority," Greek *exousia*, used to describe Jesus, who "taught with authority" (Matthew 7:28–29) and "by what authority…?" (Matthew 21:23–27 and Luke 5:20–24). The Preacher commands to keep considering, keep being attentive, and imitate (same word as in 6:12) their (the leaders') faith; imitate that level of faith and their conduct even when considering the results of that faith.

We remember, again, the Hebrew Christians were looking to return to the familiarity of the temple sacrifices. But Jesus, the object of the faith of those who led us, is the same eternally past, present, and eternally future. The new covenant is better than the old. Don't be carried away by varied and strange (Greek *poimaino* meaning "various features" and *xenos* meaning "alien") teachings. Grace is beautiful to us now ("it is good" is the Greek *kalos* meaning "good, excellent in its nature and characteristics, and therefore well adapted to its ends, praiseworthy, noble; beautiful by reason of purity of heart and life, and hence praiseworthy"[126]). We benefit by grace now where the old sacrificial system and its "various features" (animal sacrifices and all of the practices that go along with it) benefited no one. It purified no one.

Do you really want to seek comfort "inside the walls?" the Preacher is basically asking. That's not where our (Christians) altar is, and in fact, those who serve the temple "have no right to eat at our altar!" The point made of the sacrifices can be considered first, that after the animal's blood is sprinkled in the Holy of Holies, the carcass is burned (destroyed) outside of the temple area. We remember, too, that this is repeated annually. Second, Jesus sacrificed Himself outside the temple area. We are sanctified by His blood, which He shed once for all "outside the gate."

It's as if the Preacher is asking the Christians at this point, "Where do you really want to be?" If we remember and imitate the faith of our leaders, which resulted in their conduct of persevering, even dying, for the sake of Christ; if we remember that the old covenant has been replaced by the new covenant and that it is grace by which we are made perfect; if we remember that Jesus's sacrifice is once for all and not performed annually by priests sprinkling the blood of animals on an altar in a place where we were forbidden to go; if we are

---

126 James Strong, *The New Strong's Expanded Dictionary of Bible Words* (Thomas Nelson Publishers, 2001), page 1162.

looking for the city that is to come and realize that we are not citizens of this present place; then can we Christians really find comfort and peace back within the temple?

Hence ("because of the preceding premise" or "for this reason"[127]), we Christians go to Jesus "outside the camp bearing His reproach." The word "bearing" comes from the Greek word *phero*, and in all the words from the original language we have viewed in this study, I believe the Preacher saved this best for last. It is a word that doesn't merely mean that one will bear or carry a load, for example. It is a word picture of one "moved or impelled," not acting on his or her impulses but, as in this case, being "borne along by the Holy Spirit's power."[128]

Christ suffered. Those who led us suffered. We, by the Holy Spirit's power, will persevere and bear suffering for Christ. Sacrifices will be made, but not animal sacrifices. In fact Jesus's sacrifice is once for all. Rather our continual unashamed sacrifice will be our verbal praise for God and giving thanks to who He is in His entirety. Our conduct and sacrifices will demonstrate our joy, our exceedingly delight to honor God, through Jesus Christ, by the power of the Holy Spirit. This pleases (Greek *euaresteo* meaning "gratifies entirely!"[129]) God!

---

127 *The American Heritage College Dictionary* (Houghton Mifflin Company, 4th edition, 2004), page 646.
128 James Strong, *The New Strong's Expanded Dictionary of Bible Words* (Thomas Nelson Publishers, 2001), page 1437.
129 Ibid, page 1116.

You see, Christians, we don't seek to deny being persecuted. Rather, it is our faith in Christ that results in conduct that the world does not accept or understand. We are exceedingly delighted to allow the Holy Spirit to move us, equip us, toward that to which God our Heavenly Father is entirely gratified!

Benediction

Hence, the Preacher urges the brethren to "bear with" (Greek *anechomai* meaning to "endure"[130]) his words of "solace" ("exhortation" is from the Greek word *paraklesis*, a word picture of one coming to one's side to comfort[131]). With the Preacher's last words, we understand his message was one delivered to Christians, as only Christians would understand and appreciate his conclusion, "*Grace* be with you all!"

Amen!

May the grace of Christ our Savior
And the love of God our Father
And the fellowship of the Spirit
Be with us forever,
And ever,
Forevermore! [132]

---

130 Ibid, page 956.
131 Ibid, page 1290.
132 Hymn by Tome Fettke, "Grace, Love, and Fellowship." © 1986 by Word Music from *The Baptist Hymnal*, Convention Press, 1991, number 661.

CPSIA information can be obtained at www.ICGtesting.com
Printed in the USA
BVOW05s0314230315

392788BV00001B/3/P